IBSEN: THE MAN AND HIS WORK

IBSEN:
THE MAN AND
HIS WORK

By

Edvard Beyer

Translated by Marie Wells

TAPLINGER PUBLISHING COMPANY
New York

First published in the United States in 1980 by
TAPLINGER PUBLISHING CO., INC.
New York, New York

Copyright © 1978 by J. W. Cappelens Forlag
Translation copyright © 1978 by Souvenir Press and Marie Wells

Library of Congress Cataloging in Publication Data

Beyer, Edvard, 1920-
  Ibsen, the man and his work.

  Bibliography: p.
  1. Ibsen, Henrik, 1828-1906—Criticism and interpretation. I. Title.
PT8895.B4413   1980   839.8'2'26   79-1917
          ISBN 0-8008-4055-0
       ISBN 0-8008-4056-9 (pbk.)

Acknowledgment

The translation of the second version of 'Building Plans' on page 85 is taken from E. F. Garrett's *Lyrics and Poems from Ibsen*, and is quoted by kind permission of J. M. Dent & Sons Ltd.

Contents

A Background Sketch

For the greater part of his creative life, Henrik Ibsen lived away from the country of his birth, in Italy and Germany. He followed with interest the European events of the period, and European cultural life and literature made a deep impression on him. The road to world fame began on the stages of Germany, but his original background was a small, provincial town in a small, and in many ways backward, country; and the Norwegian provincial town was to be the setting of many of his best known plays. His first literary impressions he received from older Norwegian and Danish writers, but of his contemporaries the one who stimulated him most was, without doubt, his Norwegian colleague Bjørnstjerne Bjørnson. If as a young man, Ibsen half fled to wider fields, he nevertheless remained actively interested in everything that went on at home, and despite geographic distance nearly all his work stands in a strong and intimate relationship to the Norway of his day. He could be uncompromising, negative and merciless in his criticism, but he always felt that he was involved in the fate of his country and people, 'for one is never quite without responsibility and guilt in relation to the society to which one belongs' (letter 1880). Thus there are important sides of his writing which can best be understood if one knows something about the society and literature to which it is most immediately related.

Ibsen's Norway

Ibsen's life stretched from 1828 to 1906, and coincides with a significant period in Norway's political, social and cultural history. Fourteen years before he was born, in the last phase of the Napoleonic wars, the country had been ceded by the Danish king to the Swedish king. But in a short interlude in the spring of 1814 the Norwegians had succeeded in creating their own very liberal constitution, and in laying the foundations for relative independence within the new Swedish-Norwegian union. The country acquired its own constitutional apparatus – *storting* (parliament), government and supreme court – and its own capital, Christiania (Oslo since 1925). For the whole of the rest of the century, Norway's political history is characterized by the stubborn struggle to defend, secure and extend self-government and to strengthen its independence in relation to Sweden – its partner in the union – and the Swedish king. Several times the struggle came to a dramatic head, and it ended in 1905 (the year before Ibsen died), with Norway breaking away from the union.

This struggle is intimately connected with economic, social, and internal political developments. When Ibsen was born, Norway was still an almost medieval agrarian society. Of a population of approximately one million, between 80% and 90% were involved in agriculture, either as owners, tenant farmers, crofters or labourers. The country had no upper class in the European sense – no nobility, only a handful of landowners and mill- and mineowners. The leading class was the *embetsklasse* or official class, which not only included the upper ranks of the administration, judiciary, army and navy, but also the clergy, professors at the university (started in 1813) and teachers in the state-controlled secondary schools. But round about 1850, when Ibsen was writing his first play, this society was beginning to change character. It was the period when the first factories were founded, and the authorities were creating conditions for the rapid development of a capitalist economy.

Laws were liberalized, and the widely scattered parts of the country were linked together with the help of railways, coastal ferries, roads, post and telegraph systems. Fisheries, trade and shipping began to expand (the merchant fleet increased six-fold between 1850 and 1880), and agriculture was slowly modernized. By the mid-1870s, when Ibsen had begun to write his modern social dramas, Norway had largely reached the same technical and economic level as other western European countries. The population had risen to more than two million despite emigration to America, and an increasingly large proportion lived in the towns. In 1845 the capital had somewhat over 25,000 inhabitants, in the mid-1890s about 180,000. And the towns were more and more populated by new social groups: a large, poor and powerless working class, a well-to-do and expanding middle class, the new upper class, and a more fluid petit bourgeois class of independent tradesmen, craftsmen, lawyers, sea captains and private and public officials of various sorts.

Those who wrote the constitution in 1814 were predominantly men from the official class, but they realized that in the long run, political independence would have to rest on a broader and more solid foundation, and so the constitution contained clauses about franchise and eligibility for office which opened the way to political influence for the freehold farmers, the backbone of the Norwegian farming community. Despite this, it was the official class which retained control, and during its golden age it felt itself inspired and justified by its leadership of the nation and by its understanding of the common good. But its social horizons were limited, and from the 1830s onwards the farmers began seriously to pursue their own policies both at national and local level.

In the wake of the 1848 revolutionary uprisings in continental Europe there also appeared in Norway a non-parliamentary, radical-democratic reform movement, led by

Marcus Thrane – and with Henrik Ibsen among its sympathizers and helpers. The Thranites defended the cause of the crofters and workers and acquired many supporters in central parts of the country, but were then brutally suppressed. A split occurred in the farming opposition over this issue, but towards the end of the 1860s an alliance was made between the remaining majority of the farmers' opposition and representatives of the petit bourgeois and the liberal section of the middle class. This is the historical background to Ibsen's political comedy, *The League of Youth* (1869). On the other side, the official class, the wealthy farmers and the greater part of the middle class united to defend the status quo. To an increasing extent the conservatives looked to the union with Sweden and to the monarchy for support, while the democratic opposition asserted their demands for national independence all the more vigorously.

These struggles reached their climax at the beginning of the 1880s, and reverberations may be heard in *Ghosts*, *An Enemy of the People* and *Rosmersholm*. At the elections in 1882, the alliance of the left won an overwhelming victory, and in 1884 it formed a government. With this the seventy-year-old rule of the official class was replaced by the rule of the parliamentary majority. At the same time, both sides organized themselves into official parties, *Høyre* (Conservative) and *Venstre* (Liberal). In the Conservative party the upper middle class increasingly took over control from the official class, while conflicts began to split the Liberals who had been united while in opposition. At the same time the Liberals tried to defend themselves against the 'lower ranks'.

The change of government in 1884 was a political breakthrough for the middle classes, both in the country districts and in the towns, and an important step in a democratic direction, but no more than that. The great majority of the people had no political influence, and the Norwegian Labour Party, which was founded in 1887, had little chance to be heard. In the decades which followed, Conservatives and Liberals were alternately in power, but neither of them showed the slightest inclination or ability to solve the important socio-political problems. People were more and more preoccupied by conflicts arising out of the union with Sweden, and it was a united *Storting* and a Conservative–Liberal coalition government which finally made the break with Sweden.

The literary environment

Almost no Norwegian literature appeared during the four hundred years when Norway was united with Denmark. Norwegian-born writers, and Ludvig Holberg (1684–1754), the great comedy writer, first and foremost, had contributed significantly to what a later period has tended to call the *dansk-norske felleslitteratur* (Dano-Norwegian literature), and in their use of language and their portrayal of nature, several had revealed distinctly Norwegian features. But it was not until after 1814 that the desire to create a truly national literature began to make itself felt.

At that time romanticism was in full bloom in Denmark and Sweden. Here it is necessary to mention only the Danish poet Adam Oehlenschläger (1779–1850), whose historical tragedies were to be important for the saga dramas of Bjørnson and Ibsen. We also find certain romantic characteristics in the minor Norwegian writers, who in the period following 1814 wrote grandly about the greatness of ancient Norway and the freedom of the new Norway. Among these was the prolific short-story writer, Maurits Hansen (1794–1842). His retrospective unravelling technique and frequently bizarre characters presumably provided some of the inspiration for Ibsen's plays. But the conditions for literary life were very poor. The first professional theatre was not opened until 1827, and then the majority of actors were Danish. Despite this, the country shortly after gave birth to its first writer of stature, Henrik Wergeland (1808–45). He made his debut the year after Ibsen was born and died before Ibsen reached manhood. He was primarily a lyric poet, but he was also a dramatist, prose writer, educationist, historian and politician. His philosophy of life was romantic, and in his intellectual world romanticism, rationalism and radical liberalism merged in the same way as they did for Shelley (whom he knew only by name). He was both a cosmopolitan and fiery patriot, the first great spokesman for political equality with Sweden and for cultural liberation from the Danish hegemony.

Cultural self-awareness was given a new boost in the mid-1840s when a number of scholars began to collect and publish folklore material such as ballads, folktales, legends and folk melodies which were still very much alive in the remoter districts. At the same time historians began to do research into the inner continuity of the life of the people right through the Danish period and back to the Old Norse time of greatness, the saga period. The brilliant philologist Ivar Aasen (1813–96) indicated a close connection between the dialects of the interior part of the country and Old Norse, the language of the sagas, and on the basis of the most primitive or unchanged dialects, he in the 1850s created a new common denominator *landsmål* (later called *nynorsk*). This was an alternative to the traditional written language which was still Danish, but which was now becoming more open to infusions from the living colloquial speech of town and country than it had been before. It was in line with this national movement that the violin virtuoso Ole Bull in 1850 founded *Det norske Theater* in Bergen, which was only to use Norwegian actors and Norwegian pronunciation. Two years later a corresponding theatre was founded in the capital. Ibsen came to be closely involved with them both, and to gain basic experience from working with them.

The National Renaissance, as it has been called, also

opened new sources of inspiration for Norwegian art and literature. In this connection mention should be made of Johan Sebastian Welhaven (1807–73), who at one time had been Wergeland's bitterest enemy. His technically assured national romantic poems inspired the young Ibsen. The youthful works of Ibsen and Bjørnson – the saga dramas in particular – as well as the music of Edvard Grieg would be inconceivable without the National Renaissance.

But the romantic preoccupation with the traditions of the nation could also be an evasion of the seriousness of life and the problems of the day. It was the voice of Søren Kierkegaard (1813–55) in Denmark which spoke of the seriousness of living. In books such as *Either – Or* (1843) and *Stages on Life's Way* (1845) he brought man face to face with the ultimate existential choice, as later Ibsen's Brand was also to face it. And in his polemical work *Øieblikket* (*The Moment*), he directed a scathing attack on the church and official Christianity, an attack which leads one to think both of Brand and of Pastor Manders in *Ghosts*, as well as of many other clerical caricatures in the Norwegian literature of the 1880s.

Camilla Collett (1813–95), Wergeland's sister, was a writer of a totally different type. In *Amtmandens Døttre* (*The Sheriff's Daughters*), which was written between 1854 and 1855 and which was the first novel in Norway to deal with a social problem, she described the oppressed position of women, and with talent and passion asserted their right to control their own lives. Threads run from this work to Ibsen's *Love's Comedy*, and from her later feminist propaganda works to *A Doll's House*.

Throughout the entire period there was a lively literary exchange among the Scandinavian countries, and particularly between Denmark and Norway. From the beginning of the 1860s the leading Norwegian writers had their works published by Gyldendal in Copenhagen, and as many were sold and read in Denmark as in Norway. The Norwegian desire for self-assertion did not stop people – particularly in academic and literary circles – from being warm supporters of Scandinavian solidarity; on the contrary, many believed like Ibsen that the most enthusiastic Norwegian patriots, 'the Norwegian Norsemen', were also the best Scandinavianists. Thus when Denmark was attacked by Germany in 1863, and the Norwegian and Swedish politicians found it ill-advised to plunge their countries into war, this was the death blow not only for 'Scandinavianism', but also for the national romantic ideology, which Ibsen as much as anyone had believed in and used as a source of inspiration in his writing.

The Danish-German war thus brought national romanticism and the saga dramas to a sudden end and it hastened 'the modern breakthrough' in Scandinavian literature. Again the inspiration came from Denmark: in the autumn of 1871 Georg Brandes (1842–1927) began a series of lectures at the University of Copenhagen about main currents in the European literature of the nineteenth century, and these were soon published in book form. In his introduction he launched a fierce attack on Scandinavian late romanticism and its remoteness from reality, and created slogans for a modern literature that was to be socially critical and concerned about problems of the period. Both here and elsewhere he directed the attention of his Scandinavian literary colleagues to modern European literature. He became the most important mediator of newer trends of thought, such as positivism, utilitarianism, the emancipation of women and the radical biblical criticism of Feuerbach and others. These ideas formed the ideological basis for the realistic and critical literature of 'the modern breakthrough' of the 1870s and 1880s and became a powerful weapon against the old holders of power and the established society.

The reaction to this was not slow in coming. As early as

1874, students at the university matriculation ceremony were warned against dangerous modern ideas. The speaker, Professor E. F. Lochmann, even went so far as to suggest an intellectual 'quarantine' which would keep infectious foreign material away. The more literature was influenced by modern ideas, the more strongly it was condemned, not only by the critics, but also by other spokesmen for the status quo, not least by the clergy. Never has Norwegian literature faced stronger opposition, but never has it had more enthusiastic readers either. It was a force to be reckoned with in the period, a political force, and both critics and other readers adopted positions based on political considerations.

'The modern breakthrough' was a golden age for literature in Norway. It was then, with their contemporary plays, that both Bjørnson and Ibsen reached beyond the boundaries of Scandinavia. It was at this time too that a number of significant writers, Jonas Lie (1833–1908), Kristian Elster (1841–81), Amalie Skram (1846–1905), Alexander Kielland (1849–1906) and Arne Garborg (1851–1924) created the modern Norwegian novel.

The reading public to which the literature of the modern breakthrough mainly appealed came from the liberal bourgeoisie and petit bourgeoisie. But gradually, as the writers became sharper in their criticism and extended their social horizon, and as the reading public became reconciled to the social status quo and entrenched in their new positions, there sprang up an ever increasing distance and lack of trust between writer and public. The first clear sign of this was the reaction to *Ghosts* in 1881. In the mid-1880s a radical, anarchistic group of writers, the 'Christiania Bohemians', was met with open hostility both by the public and the new 'liberal' government. And the young writers who emerged round about 1890 felt themselves estranged from the public. The most representative of them, Knut Hamsun, dismissed both society and the socially critical writings of the older generation. He indicated a new field for writers: 'the strange activity of the nerves, the whisper of the blood, the entreaty of the bone, the whole unconscious life of the soul'. And he poured his sarcasms over the great writers of the age, Ibsen in particular, without showing any petty concern for the fact that Ibsen especially had shown considerable understanding of the unconscious life of the soul.

Throughout his life, no writer meant more to Ibsen than his greatest contemporary in Norwegian literature, Bjørnstjerne Bjørnson (1832–1910). They had known each other since youth, and followed each other's activity both with interest and with criticism. Bjørnson had on several occasions come to the rescue when his friend had been in difficulties. But basically different as they were, it was not always easy for them to understand each other, and for long periods misunderstandings would come between them. But time and again they would come together again. It is not putting it too strongly to say that they could not do without each other – as mutual challenge and inspiration, but also as people. 'If anything should have happened to you', Ibsen wrote once when he heard that Bjørnson had been in danger of his life, 'then all joy in my work would have slipped from me.' Only very rarely does Ibsen express himself so unreservedly in his letters.

One can hardly imagine a greater contrast than the two men. While Ibsen was introverted, shy, brooding, and preferred to concentrate on his writing, Bjørnson was extroverted, active and ready to accept a challenge – and certainly not as simple and self-confident as tradition would have him. He was a successor to Wergeland, had the emotional temperament of the born leader, played a prominent role in both the political and cultural fight for independence, and was a fearless spokesman for any individual or nation that suffered injustice. Ibsen wrote poetry in his youth, but concentrated more and more on drama; Bjørnson expressed himself in all genres, and broke new ground as a lyric poet, epic writer and dramatist. Although Ibsen was four years older and made his debut six years earlier, it was Bjørnson who first made a name for himself with his saga dramas, peasant stories and songs, and until way up in the 1860s when Ibsen's *Brand* was published it was Bjørnson who was generally considered the greater. He had a bolder approach, greater self-confidence and daring also in the field of literature, and time and again he was the pioneer even as a dramatist. He could create better crowd scenes than Ibsen, but he rarely took time to concentrate on an individual, and he could be careless about details. Ibsen followed, took more time, penetrated to the depths of the human soul and erected dramatic structures with an unfailing architectural sense. For posterity it is easy to see that Ibsen was the greater dramatist. But it was Bjørnson with his contemporary plays who paved the way to the world's great theatres.

Today, the fact that it was Bjørnson and not Ibsen who received the Nobel Prize for literature (1903) is regarded as evidence of how little literary prizes are really worth. But at the time things looked different. Since then Ibsen's position has grown stronger and stronger, and today he stands as one of the great dramatists of all time, while Bjørnson is forgotten outside Scandinavia and some of the Slavonic countries. But from a literary-historical point of view, they are inseparable.

Henrik Ibsen: The Man and his Work

Excluded from polite society

In the eighteenth and nineteenth centuries the majority of Norwegian writers were of official-class background (see p. 8). A few were the sons of farmers and crofters. Henrik Johan Ibsen, on the other hand, came from burgher stock on both sides. He was born in Skien, a shipping and sawmill town with a population of a few thousand, on 20 March 1828, and his parents belonged to a closed circle of well-to-do skippers and merchants, who set the tone of the town. But when the boy, the eldest of five brothers and sisters, was seven years old, his father's complicated business affairs collapsed. Their large house in town, 'Stockmannsgården', was sold and the family moved out to the farm 'Venstøp', where they lived in modest circumstances. In the class-conscious society of the day, such *déclassement* was regarded as shameful and that presumably goes a little of the way towards explaining that need for restitution which came to characterize the writer. But it also gave him some of the out-cast's freedom in relation to the established classes.

At 'Venstøp' the boy was shy and withdrawn, but he got his own back in the world of the imagination, playing with a puppet theatre, conjuring, drawing and painting. He also read quite widely: the Bible, the short stories of Maurits Hansen and others in the monthly periodical *Bien*, and probably also Friedrich Schiller's tragedy *Wilhelm Tell*. Occasionally he would be allowed to accompany his mother

1   The earliest known portrait of Ibsen dates from *c.* 1860.
He was then thirty-two years old, and had already written
several plays, been stage director at the Norwegian Theatre in
Bergen and director of the Christiania Norwegian Theatre.

2   The farm Venstøp in Gjerpen near Skien, Ibsen's childhood home from the age of seven to fifteen. Detail of a drawing by Arent Christensen. Venstøp which had been the family's summer residence had to be sold when Ibsen's father went bankrupt, but the family continued to rent accommodation there.

to see the travelling theatre companies which every so often visited Skien and performed French and Danish comedies and vaudevilles.

Round about Christmas 1843 he was sent to Grimstad to become an apprentice to an apothecary. This was a very wretched time for him, and things were not made any better when, at eighteen years old, he had a son by one of the servant girls in the house. For many years after, a large part of the little he earned had to go in payment for the fostering of his child. Perhaps the sexual fear and reticence which is often evident in his works is in part attributable to this experience. He worked hard, however, took his apothecary assistant's examination, and with the aim of studying medicine, began on his own to prepare himself for the matriculation examination. He also became one of a small and cheerful group of friends, wrote satirical verse about local dignitaries and took part in some high-spirited pranks, but still found time to read – among other things Shakespeare, the tragedies of the Danish poet Oehlenschläger, and perhaps even some of the works of Sören Kierkegaard. With great enthusiasm he immersed himself in Voltaire, and could shock both his friends and worthy citizens with his Voltairian maxims, his attacks on marriage, on current morality, on religion and society, his enthusiasm for the revolutions of 1848. He would also read aloud for his friends the poems he had written – perhaps even a whole tragedy.

First poetic attempts and dramatic debut

The earliest of Ibsen's poems to be preserved is one called 'Resignation', dated 1847, which touches on a theme that was to reappear in his writings to the end, namely doubt about his calling. But Ibsen did not resign. On the contrary, 'Resignation' is the first poem in a planned collection, *Miscellaneous Verse – From the Years 1848, 1849, 1850*, which he had intended to have printed. In verse form, imagery, choice of words and expression there are strong echoes from the poets of the time, first and foremost Welhaven, but also Oehlenschläger, to whom he pays tribute in a memorial poem, Heine and Wergeland. The motifs and moods are typical of the time, but they also have a personal colour. Moreover the poems have a distinctive note of their own, for the fear and loneliness which strike us give the impression of being genuine and deeply felt. The budding dramatist swings between opposites, as in 'Doubt and Hope' where he speaks of his lost childhood faith. The restless striving which was to fill so many of his characters finds expression in 'An Evening Walk in the Woods': 'No peace in life, no peace in the grave, / no peace in eternity'. Often he looks back on days that are gone, hopes which have failed, but in the temple of remembrance the memory lives eternally young; it is pure Welhaven, but also looks forward to *Love's Comedy*.

There are also extrovert, political poems, inspired by the

3   One of the first days of January 1844, the fifteen-year-old Henrik Ibsen arrived at the house of the apothecary Reimann in Grimstad to become his apprentice. At the beginning of 1847 the apothecary was taken over by a new owner who moved the store to a new house. This picture shows Ibsen's room there, where according to tradition he wrote *Catiline* in 1848/49.

revolutions of 1848–49. 'To Hungary!' acclaims the Hungarian rebels who were fighting against long odds, but whom Ibsen exhorted to take strength from the knowledge that freedom fighters all over the world were fighting the same battle. In 'Scandinavians Awake!' he rebukes 'the Norwegian and Swedish brothers' for their betrayal of Denmark, as he was to do again half a generation later, though now with far from the same poetic force.

Ibsen wrote his first tragedy during the winter of 1848–49. His friends were enthusiastic, and one of them tried to get it accepted by Christiania Theatre and published by a publisher, but in vain, and in the end the friend paid for the printing himself. It appeared on 12 April 1850, *Catiline – A Drama in Three Acts* by Brynjolf Bjarme. The edition was of 250 copies, forty-five of which were sold in the course of a year. As to performance, that did not take place till 1881 – in Stockholm.

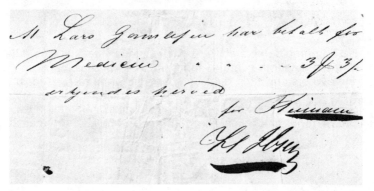

4   A receipt of payment for medicine, signed by Ibsen on behalf of the apothecary Reimann (Ibsen Museum, Grimstad).

In the preface to the second edition (1875), Ibsen has himself pointed to the topical background for the play – the February Revolution, the Hungarian uprising, the war in Schleswig – as well as his personal 'state of war with the tiny community where I was confined by the conditions of my life and by circumstances'. In this context he became preoccupied with the Roman rebel Catiline, whom he met in two of the set texts for his matriculation exam, Sallust and

5   Shipping dominated the town life of Grimstad in the middle of the nineteenth century, and polite society was made up of shipowners and their families. Ibsen had little respect for the citizens of the town, indeed, felt he was in a state of war with the tiny community, and mocked its inhabitants in caricatures and lampoons. The photograph shows Storgaten in Grimstad in about 1860.

Cicero. However, he treated the historical material very freely, almost 'as a vehicle for the underlying idea of the play' as he wrote in a postscript.

The drama shows the influence of many and fine masters. The atmosphere of revolt as well as certain elements in the hero's fate remind one of Schiller's *Die Räuber*; details of the plot and dialogue of Shakespeare's *Julius Cæsar*, *Hamlet* and *Macbeth*; while the poetic metre, blank verse for the most part, reminds one chiefly of Oehlenschläger's historical plays. Many scenes are melodramatic, and character portrayal is superficial, despite all the spiritual conflict, while the language often sounds hollow and bombastic. But a feeling for conflict, suspense and climax reveal the born dramatist, and many central Ibsen motifs make their first appearance here. This is true of 'the conflict between ability and aspiration, between will and possibility', as he himself mentions in the preface to the second edition, but it is also true of the conflict between calling and the desire for happiness. And when the hero stands between two contrasting types of woman, who speak to the opposing forces in his soul, when he is overtaken and struck down by his own secret guilt, represented by the avenger Furia, and when despite this his soul is perhaps saved by the love of the gentle Aurelia – these are all characteristics which point to future developments in the authorship. The treatment of the historical material is also characteristic. Ibsen looks at the rebel with far greater sympathy than his sources do, but the social and political aspects of the matter have almost disappeared. Catiline's revolt is the revolt of the individual against the powerful, he carries defeat within him, and the most important conflict is the spiritual one:

> Is not life, then, an unending battle
> between the opposing forces of the soul, –
> and this battle is the soul's own life ...

One of the few who despite many reservations saw something promising in 'Brynjolf Bjarme', was the philosopher and critic, M. J. Monrad. Here was someone who began 'from within, from the idea', and 'where this stirs powerfully, one may be sure that it will eventually find its form'. The idea, 'the beautiful main idea of the poem', was an obvious affirmation of 'the established moral order' *against* 'the individual's vague urge for independence', according to Monrad. In this, one may assume, he was on the wrong track.

Apprenticeship years and National Romanticism

In the spring of 1850 Ibsen left Grimstad, visited his parents – whom he was never to see again – and then travelled on to the capital. He enrolled immediately at Heltberg's student crammer, and took his matriculation exam in August, but he failed two subjects and did not resit them, so could not matriculate and study. Shortly after however, on 26 September 1850, the Christiania Theatre gave the first of all Ibsen premières. It was of *The Warrior's Barrow – A Dramatic Work in One Act* by Brynjolf Bjarme.

Catilina,

Drama i tre Acter,

af

Brynjolf Bjarme.

———•••◆•••———

Christiania.

J Kommission hos P. F. Steensballe.

F. Steens Bogtrykkeri.

1850.

6   The title-page of the first edition of *Catiline*, A Play by Brynjolf Bjarme, published in Christiania in 1850. The book was sold on commission by P. F. Steensballe, but the cost of printing the 250 copies had been borne by Ole Schulerud, Ibsen's good friend in Grimstad. Approximately 45 copies were sold, then Ibsen and Schulerud sold the remainder as wrapping paper one day when they were short of cash.

The play deals with one of Oehlenschläger's favourite themes, the meeting between paganism and Christianity, north and south. The action takes place in Normandy, and the plot is tortuous, but ends with the reconciliation of differences through love, and the play closes with a prophecy of national rebirth and new heroic deeds in the distant future – a future at present visible only on 'the silver-blue sea of thought'. The play appealed to the national-romantic taste of the time, but in all respects must be regarded as inferior to *Catiline*.

As a lyric poet, however, Ibsen was growing. With A. O. Vinje[1] and Paul Botten Hansen[2] he produced the tiny paper

7 Bundling. Satirical drawing in *Andhrimner* presumably by Ibsen. The boy wants to come in, but Marit protests that she has to consider her friend Ola. 'Ola?', he says, 'that dolt is hardly likely to have the time or inclination to come to the mountain farm now, because he has – well, let me in first, dear kind Marit, and then I'll tell you all about it.'

[1] Vinje was a journalist and poet who wrote in *New Norwegian*.
[2] Botten Hansen a literary critic and editor. (Tr.)

Andhrimner, and among the many poems by 'Brynjolf Bjarme' which appeared in it during the spring and summer of 1851 was one, 'The Miner', which even in its original version was well on the way to becoming the most Ibsenian of all poems. The theme of the miner is one that many had treated before, and both vocabulary and metre bear a strong resemblance to 'The Miner's Song' by Maurits Hansen. But Ibsen has made the motif his own, a symbol of the irresistible, fated quest for understanding which drives him to the depths. The ability to find simple and potent images for spiritual experiences also characterizes several other poems which in a more or less revised form were later to find their way into Ibsen's only collection of poems.

Ibsen also wrote theatre reviews in *Andhrimner*, and in these was strongly influenced by the theories of the Danish critic and writer J. L. Heiberg. He demanded respect for the distinctive qualities of the various genres and vigorously asserted that art should unite the 'ideal' and the 'real': not simply represent reality, but carry it within itself. In political articles and commentaries he was sarcastic about weak members of the opposition in the *Storting* (parliament), and they were ridiculed even more in a short opera-parody, *Norma or A Politician's Love*. It is a mere bagatelle, but contains elements which were to come to full flowering in *The League of Youth*. At the same time he was active in the Thrane movement, took part in meetings and demonstrations, helped the editor of *Arbeider-Foreningernes Blad*, Theodor Abildgaard, to write political songs, and taught at the association's school for adults. In the summer of 1851 when the police struck out at the movement, Ibsen only just managed to escape arrest.

Some months later Ibsen became attached to the Norwegian Theatre which Ole Bull had recently founded in Bergen. He was to 'assist the theatre as dramatic author', and write at least one new play per year for the anniversary of its foundation on 2 January. Soon after he was also made 'stage director' – i.e. he was to be responsible for that part of the directing which concerned the characters' movements on stage.

The theatre management was generous and liberal-minded enough to send him to Denmark and Germany to study acting, and in Copenhagen and Dresden he was able to watch first class actors in both classical and modern dramas. He met leading theatre people; in Copenhagen he saw the brilliant Johanne Luise Heiberg in several major roles, as he was to recall eighteen years later in one of his most beautiful poems (see p. 92), and in Dresden he was able to familiarize himself with new, more realistic forms of staging. But his most lasting benefit from the journey was probably the discovery of a little book, *Das moderne Drama*, by the German literary historian, Hermann Hettner. We shall never know whether, or to what extent, Ibsen's work would have been different if he had never read *Das moderne Drama*. But here were certainly thoughts on historical tragedy, bourgeois drama and modern comedy which he was to put into practice in the years to come.

On his travels Ibsen wrote *St John's Night*, a fairytale comedy like Shakespeare's *A Midsummer Night's Dream* and Oehlenschläger's *St John's Eve Play*, but coloured by Norwegian national romanticism. The dream-vision which reveals the truth to those who really can *see*, comes very close to the folksong about Little Kjersti. But the reaction to the dream-vision also exposes the false and superficial kind of national romanticism, which is represented by the verbose man-of-letters, Julian Poulsen. This satirical portrait of one of the types of the period is the first faint prefiguring of such characters as Peer Gynt, Stensgård and Hjalmar Ekdal.

The performance was a fiasco, and the text was not printed until Ibsen's posthumous papers were published. However, *Lady Inger of Østråt*, a play that was ready for performance on 2 January 1855, was of a totally different

calibre. It is an historical character tragedy, but with a
message to the age – and to that extent in accord with
Hettner's demands. But it is also Ibsen's first significant
drama.

How did Norway come under foreign domination? Could
it have retained its old independence – and, implied in that,
could it regain it? These were questions which many people
pondered over during the period of 'national renaissance'
and smouldering national assertiveness in relation to Sweden,
which was soon to flare up into conflict over the post of
the viceregent. The historian P. A. Munch had maintained
that Fru Ingerd Ottesdatter of Austråt ought to have led an
uprising, and in 1854 there appeared a Danish work
about 'the count's feud', which mentioned her unsuccessful
attempts in 1527–28. Ibsen saw dramatic possibilities in the
character and material, studied the sources thoroughly, but
used them very freely as far as individuals and events are
concerned, and concentrated everything into one stormy
night at 'Østeraad' in the year 1528. As in *Catiline*, he
interprets events from an idealistic and individualistic view
of history. Everything depends on the leader's faithfulness
to his calling.

Lady Inger has never doubted that she has been chosen
by God to fight as 'heaven's tool' for 'the divine cause', the
freedom of her country. But her sense of vocation and the
needs of the people wrestle with strong forces within her:
maternal love and the desire for human happiness. She has
an illegitimate son whom no one knows about, and he is the
only living reminder of the short period in her life when she
felt herself fully to be a woman. Concern for his safety binds
her hand and foot; she cannot act, and when the cunning
Danish agent, Niels Lykke, demands a clear statement of
her position, she is forced to resort to intrigues which
involve both the future of Norway and her son's life. Her
wavering between the two considerations becomes fateful. It

8   Lady Inger of Østråt (Agnes Mowinckel) whispers to Olaf Skaktavl (Oscar Leffmann), 'Now I know for certain – Niels Lykke is a traitor!' From Act IV of *Lady Inger of Østråt* at the Central Theatre, Oslo, during the Ibsen centenary in 1928.

is with terrible irony that her dissimulation and double dealing finally recoil on the son for whom she has sacrificed everything, but thereby also on her and the cause she has been called to serve.

The plot is exceedingly complicated, and its construction is heavily influenced by the French dramatic writer, Scribe, with whose technique Ibsen was as a director himself thoroughly familiar. Hettner had warned against using dramatic 'tricks' unless they were determined by the psychology of the characters. But here, to a large extent, they are so justified. Double dealing has become part of Fru Inger's nature and by vacillating and hesitating she has let herself become the victim of chance. It is true that every so often the complicated intrigues threaten to overshadow her spiritual conflict, but time and again her inner struggle

9   The final scene of *Lady Inger of Østråt*. Soldiers come into the hall of Østråt, carrying the body of Nils Stenssøn, Lady Inger's son. Illustration in *Illustreret Nyhedsblad*, in which the play appeared as a serial in the summer of 1857.

breaks through with compelling force. She is Ibsen's first significant character study.

The action is condensed. It reaches a peak towards the end of each act, and a turning point in the third, but continues to increase in intensity right up to a sudden reversal in the very last scene. There is a variation on the theme of Lady Inger's memory of her youth, in the secondary plot between her daughter Eline and Niels Lykke. But the 'unity of time and place' are strictly adhered to, and in this Ibsen moves away from the dominant Shakespearean tradition and approaches the classical. In the dialogue on the other hand he distinguishes himself not only from Shakespeare and Oehlenschläger, but from the classical tradition also, in that he uses prose in a historical tragedy – a dramatic prose, moving and grand, but without any attempt at pastiche.

Not even this play was a success. Botten Hansen printed

it in *Illustreret Nyhedsblad*, however, and it was published as a special issue. A play that was a success with the public, and to some extent with the critics also, was the folksong drama, *The Feast at Solhoug* (1856). *Olaf Liljekrans* (1857), a play in the same genre, met with a cool reception.

Folksong drama was a genre that was much cultivated in Denmark, especially by Henrik Hertz, but Ibsen found the most important motifs in Landstad's *Norwegian Folksongs* from 1853. But he made them more rationalistic: Margit 'is lured into the mountain' because she is married to an old man; Olaf Liljekrans has not danced with the fairies, but he has met the mountain girl Alfhild, who is of flesh and blood. The dialogue alternates between verse and prose. The metre is that of the folksongs, and both verse and prose are strongly influenced by the folksong language, but by Danish songs more than Norwegian ones. Both plays have considerable poetic charm, but are chiefly of interest because of the national romantic mood which they express, and because characters, groupings and motifs point to future developments in Ibsen's works. The passionate Margit is a precursor of such 'demonic' characters as Hjørdis in *The Vikings at Helgeland* and Rebecca West in *Rosmersholm*; and in *Olaf Liljekrans* which was never published, there are elements of plot and scenes which were to appear again in *Peer Gynt*.

The Feast at Solhoug was soon to be the butt of one of Norway's most amusing parodies, *The Feast at Mœrrahaug* by Jokum Pjurre (Olaf Skavlan, 1857). There the beautiful Signe speaks in the following manner: 'Down to the rose grove I'll go / to see how their blooms are a-faring; / but the carrots and turnips won't grow, / they stand abject and staring . . .' The parody struck home, and indeed proved fatal to the genre.

In September 1857 Henrik Ibsen took over the directorship of the Christiania Norwegian Theatre. The five years in Bergen had been a hard but useful period of apprentice-ship. Ibsen had read many plays, learnt much about the theatre, and had a chance to try his own works on the stage. In other ways too they had been eventful years. His love for the sixteen-year-old Rikke Holst had inspired some of his lightest and most cheerful poems – 'Field Flowers and Potplants', 'To My Auricula', 'A birdsong' and 'Wanderer's Song'. The affair came to an end, however, because he was coward enough to run away when they met her father. Shortly after he wrote 'In the Picture Gallery', a melancholy cycle of poems, mainly in sonnet form, about doubt and weakness confronted by the demands of art and life.

In Bergen he had also met Susanna (or Suzannah) Thoresen, the step-daughter of Magdalene Thoresen, who later became a well known writer. They became engaged in 1857 and married in 1858. To her too he wrote poetry – 'The Only One' he called her in his proposal poem – though ultimately she spoke more to the dramatist in him than to the poet. As he wrote in a long autobiographical letter to the Danish literary historian Peter Hansen in 1870, 'she is just the person I need, illogical, but with a strong poetic instinct, a high-minded way of thinking and an almost violent hatred of all petty considerations', and in a poem a year later, he says quite openly: 'Her children are / the long line of figures / who process, waving / flags through my song', ('Thanks'). The first of these 'children' was Hjørdis in *The Vikings at Helgeland*, which he wrote in the period between their engagement and their marriage.

From saga-drama to contemporary comedy

The Vikings at Helgeland is based on the fantastic and romantic legendary sagas and on the Icelandic family sagas. As he wrote later (in the foreword to the second edition of *The Feast at Solhoug*), 'what in the *Saga of the Volsungs* had been given epic form, I wanted to reproduce dramatically.'

In the main, both the prior history and the development of the plot follow the legendary Saga of the Volsungs. Hjørdis corresponds to Brynhild and like Brynhild, she has the Amazon temperament. Dagny corresponds to Gudrun, and Sigurd and Gunnar to their namesakes in the saga. But apart from that there is more of the Icelandic than of the legendary sagas in the character portrayal. Hjørdis, who is the most complex character, reminds one both of Gudrun in *The Laxdœla Saga* and Hallgerd in *Njål's Saga*. But the majority of the characters are far nobler than their saga relatives. This is particularly true of Sigurd, who turns out to be a Christian, and old Ǫrnulf, who is a very toned-down version of Egil Skallagrimsson.

10 & 11   Susanna Daae Thoresen and Henrik Ibsen became engaged in 1857, and married in Bergen on 18 June 1858. Ibsen was then director of the Christiania Norwegian Theatre, so after the wedding the couple travelled to the capital where Ibsen started his second season. The portrait of Susanna is from around 1860, the photo of Ibsen from 1861.

The play is set on the coast of Helgeland at the time of Erik Blood-Axe, and the plot covers twenty-four hours. It is far simpler than that of *Lady Inger* and the uncovering of past history has a far more direct bearing on present action. Here too misunderstandings and devices of intrigue play a part, but on the whole the dramatic structure is tauter and surer than before – as austere as the sagas themselves in fact. Both in vocabulary and sentence structure, Ibsen imitated the 'saga style' of N. M. Petersen's Danish translations. The result was admired at the time, though Bjørnson found it artificial, and today the majority would probably agree with him.

At its core, however, *The Vikings at Helgeland* has far more of Ibsen in it than it has of the sagas. Like Catiline, Sigurd stands between two opposing types of women and two opposing attitudes to life. By renouncing Hjørdis, whom he loved, for the sake of his friend, Sigurd ruined life both for himself and for her, and it is this betrayal of love which leads them both to destruction in the end. He who betrays love breaks 'the secret web of the Norns', the power of fate itself, and 'two lives are laid waste'. This idea is unknown in the sagas, but central to the play; in the sagas it is the relentlessness of fate which causes the tragedy, in Ibsen it is human betrayal and guilt.

The Vikings at Helgeland was a great success at Christiania Norwegian Theatre, where Ibsen himself directed it, but it was rejected by The Royal Theatre in Copenhagen: J. L. Heiberg found it crude and primitive. After much arguing it was also staged by the Christiania Theatre and was a great favourite of audiences there, both at the time and later. In the mid-1870s it made its triumphant way across the national boundary to the neighbouring Scandinavian countries, and to Germany and Austria.

Ibsen was full of patriotic enthusiasm when he took over the leadership of Christiania Norwegian Theatre. His aim

12   From a performance of *The Vikings at Helgeland* at Fahl-
strøms Theatre in Christiania in February 1908. Since its opening in 1899 the Norwegian National Theatre had tried to claim
the sole right to performances of Ibsen's plays in the capital.
From left to right in this scene are, Sigurd (Johan Fahlstrøm),
Ørnulf (David Lunde), Gunnar (David Knudsen) and Hjørdis
(Ragna Wettergreen).

was to foster a distinctive Norwegian theatrical tradition,
for – as he wrote – 'culture cannot be considered apart
from nationality'. And in articles, occasional verse and
polemical poems – 'Seagull Cries' and others – he cam-
paigned for his national cultural programme. He adopted
uniquely Norwegian words and forms into his language,
particularly in 'The Mountain Bird', an opera version of
Olaf Liljekrans on which he had started work. And he
persuaded Bjørnson to found The Norwegian Society, which
was to work for the national element in art and literature.
He himself was vice-president.

But the sceptic in him also claimed its due – and found it
in 'The Learned Holland Club', where Botten Hansen and
other devotees of the Danish playwright and essayist, Ludvig
Holberg, found stimulation for their thirst for knowledge,
their delight in discussion and unbridled wit. Here he found
comfort in adversity, and he needed it more and more. The

theatre was struggling with a difficult financial situation. It had sought support from the state several times, but in vain, and its director was forced to compromise his artistic and national programme, without this solving the problem. Eventually he grew tired, shirked his work, fell out with the management, was attacked in the newspapers and became involved in heated polemics. He lost heart and the desire to work – his theatrical job became, as he wrote later, 'a daily repeated act of abortion'. More than ever he doubted his vocation and his ability; he drank and was out late and almost broke down completely, but he raised himself up again. What he wrote at this time was mostly occasional verse, and the greater part of it is of little worth.

But two poems from these years, one written before the crisis, and the other perhaps just after, belong to his very best. They are the magnificent poem of ideas 'On the Heights' and the stirring verse narrative about Terje Vigen.

The first is a poetic cycle in three parts, each in a distinctive verse form. Later Ibsen divided it into nine smaller sections. The 'I' of the narrative is a country boy who goes off to the mountains to hunt, full of warm and tender thoughts for his mother and his girl in the valley. But up on the heights he meets 'the strange hunter', an enigmatic figure who slowly gains power over him, robs him of 'even the ability to will' with his seductive words about the free, heroic life up on the heights. When on Christmas Night the boy sees his mother's cottage in flames, the hunter teaches him to look 'through his hollowed hand / for the sake of the perspective' and to appreciate the æsthetic effect in the 'twofold light of night'. When on midsummer's day he sees his fiancée ride to church as someone else's bride, he no longer needs the stranger's help:

> my sail went under, my life's tree snapped,
> but see how beautifully the red of her skirt
> shines between the birch trunks.

The development which the narrator of the poem has gone through has led him from unreflecting love and earthly responsibilities to a 'higher view of things', the stance of a spectator, the price of which is 'all kinds of indications of petrifaction', though it does provide exhilaration and independence: 'up here on the heights are freedom and God,/ down there grope the others.' Some scholars believe that in this poem Ibsen has declared his own belief in the unfettered life on the heights – the æsthetic approach to life or the writer's vocation; while others maintain that he is in fact rejecting it as inhuman; and yet others conclude that he does not pass judgement, but follows a line of thought to its extreme, weighs the losses and the gains, and in the end strikes a balance between high-flown affirmation and an equally strong ironical reservation. Not least because of its teasing ambiguity, 'On the Heights' is one of Ibsen's most fascinating poems.

'Terje Vigen', which was written a couple of years later (published 1862), is of quite a different character, a narrative poem in a genuinely popular style, about the fate of a seaman 'from beginning to end'. It is associated with a dramatic period in Norwegian history, and is an exciting and moving poem, even if not totally devoid of melodramatic effects. Its human content is simple and unambiguous: it tells of Terje's ordeals and development, from the youthful urge to travel, through family responsibilities and daring enterprise, loss of everything and the gnawing desire for revenge to a liberating breakthrough of tenderness and magnanimity.

The poem is a masterpiece of composition and stands securely on its own feet. But it too grew out of what Ibsen in his letter to Peter Hansen called a life situation. The parallels are obvious. Perhaps it was precisely through the poem that he triumphed over bitterness and aggression. In any event, it expresses – as several scholars have pointed out

13   In 1913 a Swedish film company had acquired the film rights to Ibsen's works, and in 1917 *Terje Vigen* had its première. Victor Sjöström both directed the film and played the leading role. The film was an enormous success, and was shown not only throughout Europe, but also in the U.S.A., South America, and even in Africa and Asia. The illustration shows Victor Sjöström in the part of Terje Vigen. (Swedish Film Institute).

– an attitude to human responsibility which is diametrically opposed to the free life of the hunter in 'On the Heights'.

In the summer of 1862 Christiania Norwegian Theatre had to close down, and on a small grant Ibsen set off to Sogn, Nordfjord and Sunnmøre to collect legends. After that he put the finishing touches to his first dramatic work for five years, *Love's Comedy*.

Apart from *St John's Night*, this is Ibsen's first con-

temporary play. Much in it resembles the Copenhagen
student comedies of the period: the songs, the strong local
colour – 'Mrs Halm's country villa on Drammensveien' –,
the gay mood, and the contrast between Falk and the carefree
students on the one hand, and the worthy citizens and their
wives on the other. But the satire in Ibsen's comedy is
sharper and less respectful, both in its many contemporary
allusions and in its witty jibes at long engagements and
frivolous marriages.

But the ideological content lies deeper and has affinities
with the intellectual world of Kierkegaard. This is shown by
details such as the puns on the Norwegian words *kall*,
meaning both 'vocation' and 'parish', and *offer*, meaning
both 'sacrifice' and 'offertory', and by the fun poked at the
theological student's search. But it is also evident in the
central themes: in the relationship between 'the æsthetic'
and 'the ethical' in a philosophy of life and in the task of
a writer and – as Ibsen expressed it four years later – in
'the conflict between reality and the claims of the ideal,
which exists in our society in all matters concerning love
and marriage'.

'Reality' is represented by a group of amusing caricatures,
whose chief characteristics are already indicated by their
names, from the junior clerk Stiver and Miss Jay to the
clergyman Strawman with his wife and eight children. The
focal point of their conventionally excited interest is the
engagement of the boarding house landlady's youngest
daughter to the theologian, Lind. But the main plot revolves
round Svanhild, the eldest daughter, and her two suitors,
the writer, Falk, and the worldly-wise merchant, Guldstad.
Here it is a question of 'the claims of the ideal'. But it is
also a question of the relation between life and art.

Falk is one who rejoices in the present, who enjoys life and
is an æsthete, and when he asks Svanhild to belong to him
in 'God's glorious spring' it is because he wants her dreams to

nourish his song. But she calls such an attitude child's play and makes greater demands on the writer; only through his own strength and personal dedication can he create a literature which is 'life's own'. Through her resistance she calls forth deeper feelings in him, and inspired by these he makes a witty and poetic speech about tea in which he pays tribute to the love which has 'its home in the land of love', but throws scorn on 'the lie' of conventional marriages. This is the first small skirmish of the war to which he now wants to devote his strength, a war against the lie 'in the field of everyday day'. Like a modern Hjørdis and a precursor to Agnes in *Brand*, Svanhild too wants to enlist in this struggle for 'God's truth'. But Guldstad confronts them with the demands of everyday life, and against their young, romantic love sets the life-long relationship of two people. He speaks movingly of a foundation which endures beyond the period of falling in love, of kindness of heart, mutual concern and support. And Falk has to concede that *his* love is transitory. Even so it is his love that Svanhild chooses – but in its logical extreme: it is only by parting immediately, while their love is at its peak, that they can guarantee it eternal life in 'the hallowed halls of memory'. They lose each other 'for this life', but win each other 'for eternity'. In the light of memory Svanhild goes to a life of 'quiet duty', while Falk looks 'upwards' to his 'goal as poet'. But even the word 'poet' has acquired new meaning:

> As a poet, yes; for every man's a poet
> whether in parliament, in schoolroom or in church,
> every man, however great or lowly,
> who strives for the ideal in his own way.
> Yes, I go upwards; the winged steed is saddled;
> I know my task is ennobled for life.

Through love and renunciation the æsthete has become ethical. Svanhild's future path at Guldstad's side does not

have the same glorious perspective, for she pays the price
for Falk's liberation:

> Now I have finished my outdoor life;
> the leaves are falling: – let the world now take me.

The verse scheme harmonizes with the many facets of *Love's
Comedy* and follows all the changes in tone and mood, from
the lyricism and deep seriousness of the dialogues between
Svanhild and Falk, and the quiet pathos of Guldstad's most
important lines, through Falk's inflamed rhetoric and
provocative aphorisms, to the lightest tea-party conversation.
Vocabulary and manner of expression are flexible enough to
serve individual characterization: Strawman talks parsoni-
cally, Stiver officialese and Miss Jay prissily ... and while at
one moment the rhymes can clinch a paradox, at the next
they can amuse or shock with their reckless breaches of
convention.

Both the public and the critics denounced *Love's Comedy*
as immoral. Monrad was more articulate, but found the play
false, immoral and 'in an ultimate sense' unpoetical because
it presented love and marriage, ideal and reality as irreconcilable. This judgement touches the heart of the matter:
Ibsen's ideal and the reality he saw around him were so
far from each other that in a contemporary drama it was
inevitable that he would threaten the harmony which
Monrad and the 'poetic realists' demanded.

It was eleven years before the comedy was staged. But then
it went well. The times had changed.

The Pretenders – Norway's greatest saga-drama

The manner in which *Love's Comedy* had been received
made Ibsen feel that he stood alone, bereft of public understanding, and he later maintained that these feelings 'found
release' in *The Pretenders*. But the idea was old, and the
drama's immediate stimulus was an experience of an

altogether different kind, namely the huge national choral festival in Bergen in the early summer of 1863 – a characteristic expression of the period's desire for unity. Bjørnson stood out as the obvious leader of the younger generation, but he spoke warmly of his brother writer and dismissed all attempts to set the two up against each other. As soon as Ibsen arrived home again he set to work on the play about Håkon and Earl Skule and completed it in one and a half months. It was published in October the same year.

The idea of unification and the more personal problems of election and spiritual leadership are here vividly presented in impressive historical figures. Håkon has characteristics of Bjørnson, Skule of Ibsen, and yet both Håkon's consciousness of his calling and Skule's paralysing doubt about his own right have roots in the writer himself. But at the same time Ibsen has to a large extent met Hettner's demand of loyalty to one's sources – which in this case meant Sturla Tordsson's *The Saga of Håkon* and P. A. Munch's presentation in *The History of the Norwegian People*. The course of events is simplified and foreshortened. The portrayal of Håkon and Skule and the relationship between them is largely in accord with Munch. Ibsen's Bishop Nikolas, on the other hand, differs considerably from the historical one. According to the sources the bishop tried to reconcile the two rivals, but in the play he is the evil spirit who provokes and exploits the enmity between them, a schemer in the tradition of Scribe, a power-thirsty weakling akin to Shakespeare's Richard III.

In *Lady Inger of Østråt* and *The Vikings at Helgeland* Ibsen had observed the classical unities of time and place. Here, however, he reverts to the tradition of Shakespeare, with great shifts in time and place, constant changes of scene, a large gallery of figures and strongly contrasted effects. Between excited crowd scenes and bloody battle scenes, Skule exchanges profound thoughts with the bard Jatgeir about unborn songs and the gifts of sorrow and doubt – rather in the manner that Shakespeare's kings talk to their wise fools, – and immediately after the bishop's sinister death scene we hear Margaret singing her child to sleep: 'Now wall and roof are one / with the starry blue vault above'.

In *The Vikings at Helgeland* Ibsen had striven to intensify the historical colour by using the saga style. But in this play he did what shortly before he had praised Bjørnson for doing: in an enthusiastic review of Bjørnson's great historical tragedy, *Sigurd Slembe*, he said that 'he wanted to avoid an obviously historical style of language', because he 'had set himself the task of portraying a spiritual struggle which would be valid and understandable for any period'. Nor did he find it possible to write the tragedy in verse, but let the dialogue approach everyday speech, without thereby renouncing rhetorical vigour and bold images.

Håkon and Skule face each other as opposites and opponents, the one king, the other claimant to the throne, while Nikolas, at one time also a pretender, acts as Skule's evil spirit and as a dark contrast to Håkon. He personifies the lust for power which is also strong in Skule. But Skule is the main character in the tragedy. It is his craving for sovereign power, his rebellion, his success and defeat, his spiritual conflict, guilt, recognition and death which provide the main thread and the dramatic curve which leads from the first act to the fifth.

Skule is of royal descent, and has 'all the best gifts of the mind', as Håkon says. But he also has a burning desire for power, and lends a willing ear to Bishop Nikolas. However, he lacks the inner right to the kingdom, the *calling* which makes Håkon so secure. From the moment when Håkon expresses his idea of Kingship and his awareness of his calling – 'Norway was a kingdom, it shall become a people. (...) That is the task which God has laid on my shoulders' – from that moment Skule knows in his heart of hearts that Håkon is the true king. It is precisely this which drives him

14   'Now I take your pawn, my lord', Bishop Nikolas (Stein Grieg Halvorsen) to Earl Skule (Per Sunderland) in Act II of *The Pretenders*. From the Norwegian National Theatre production in 1973.

to rebel, but doubt follows him and despite his outward success it grows steadily stronger. Even in victory he is filled with a 'secret fear', and in the decisive battle he dare not – quite literally – burn his bridges behind him. Håkon's idea gains more and more power over him, and when he unexpectedly learns that he has a son, he presents it to him as his own. But the stolen royal thought possesses and poisons the son's soul and drives him, an ordained priest, to sacrilege. As a consequence of this the people turn against them, and when Skule sees what he has done to his son, he recognizes his own guilt and chooses death in order to atone and make reparation for what he has committed against Håkon. He falls by his own deeds, but he grows in defeat, gives death a meaning and dies a tragic hero. And Håkon gives him an epitaph which encompasses not only the greatness, but the mystery and pathos of the man as well: 'all men judged him wrongly (...) Skule Bårdsøn was God's stepchild on earth; that was the mystery about him'.

Håkon, on the other hand, is God's legitimate child, and is certain that the royal thought is the sign of his calling: 'The deed to be done by Norway's king, now.' He is the personification of historical necessity, 'who feels the demands of the age like a sexual passion', and who walks the path that is marked out for him and accomplishes his task. He is as certain as Skule is doubtful, indomitable in adversity, merciless when that is necessary, but conciliatory and high-minded when the time for that is ripe. Even the conflict between calling and human happiness solves itself for him. Certainly he sends away both his mother and the woman he loves – 'a king must not have anyone with him of whom he is too fond' – but he gets Margaret instead, and with her the most devoted love. Also in this he acts as a contrast to Skule, for Skule was faithless to Ingebjørg, the love of his youth, and he has been blind to his wife's love. Now he has to face what he has done to Ingebjørg, and at the end, what he has lost in relation to Ragnhild: 'I pursued love in sin and guilt, and never realized that I possessed it by virtue of the laws of God and man.' Skule betrayed love out of the lust for power, which is why judgement is also passed on his betrayal of love, while Håkon is exonerated because he sacrificed love for a higher calling.

Bishop Nikolas hates because he cannot love, cannot tolerate that others become too powerful because he himself never acquired power, and fights with cunning and intrigue because he is not capable of fighting in the open. The character is a study in the psychology of impotence and compensation, but it is also something more: the personification of envy and lust for power, a demonic force, the devil's own tool in the struggle between God's true-born child on earth and his stepchild. In him the lines from Schiller's ideologically determined character portrayal and Shakespeare's realistic-psychological character portrayal meet.

The weak point in *The Pretenders* is the scene where Nikolas's ghost makes a long speech to Skule and identifies itself with the divisive and narrow-minded spirit that will always be a threat to the life of the nation. Here the topical preaching breaks the framework of the play. Apart from this, however, the play is superbly constructed. The action is varied and exciting, but inextricably linked to the inner spiritual drama. There is a colourful gallery of characters and the social background is vivid, but everything is subordinated to the underlying conflict in the grand sweep of the whole.

In 1864 Ibsen himself staged *The Pretenders* at Christiania Theatre. It was well received by the public, was played five times – which was much in those days – and was praised as a character tragedy by Monrad. In Denmark recognition took some time to come, but it did come in 1867 when Georg Brandes wrote his first essay on Ibsen. And the drama has remained one of 'the best historical dramas of European romanticism', to quote another Danish literary scholar, Henning Fenger, one hundred years later. But it is not just as a grand historical drama and as an expression of the conflicts in Norway in the 1860s that the play is of interest. It gives valid form to a conflict which crops up again and again in political life: the barren desire for power versus the task-oriented desire to fulfill the demands of the age.

Breaking away and meeting with Italy

Ibsen's financial situation was desperate. In the autumn of 1862 his possessions were put up for auction in order to settle outstanding tax. From New Year 1863 he had a modest post as literary adviser to the Christiania Theatre. Shortly after, when Bjørnson was granted an author's stipend, Ibsen too applied for one, but the *Storting* said 'no'. However, in September of the same year he was given a small state grant for foreign travel. Bjørnson managed to raise a larger amount and on 5 April 1864 Ibsen set sail from Norway, and, apart from a couple of short visits, he stayed away for 27 years.

It had been his intention to put his efforts into a new national historical drama, this time about the free-booter Magnus Heineson, who lived at the end of the sixteenth century. But the Prussian attack on Denmark, and his anger that the Norwegians did nothing to help their kinsfolk, were to make his writing take an entirely new direction.

Ibsen had been a warm spokesman for Scandinavianism, as well as for national renaissance and unity. As early as the spring of 1861 he had promised the Danes help, should they need it: 'Surely you will receive a helping hand from us, – / but *first* from the truly *Norwegian* Norsemen!' ('Distress at Sea'). In December 1863 when the situation became serious, he warned the Norwegians against a breach of faith and goaded them to action ('To Norway!' – later called 'A Brother in Need!'). In vain. While he was in Copenhagen the defence positions at Dybbøl fell, and in Berlin he saw the Prussians' triumphal entry into the city. He continued his journey southwards and settled in Rome, but could not shake off his sorrow and his anger. In the poem 'From Dybbøl Days' – later called 'The Ground of Faith' – and in letter after letter, he dwelt on the failure of the Norwegians. He was even afraid that they had forfeited their right and ability to live as an independent nation, but he could not give up hope. It was necessary at least to put an end to the romanticization of 'our ancient history' because, as he said in a letter to Bjørnson, present Norwegians have as little in common with the old ones as the Greek pirates have with the generation which sailed to Troy and were helped by the

15   Norway's neutrality during the Danish war against the Germans in 1864 altered the Danish view of the Norwegians. Before the war Norwegian students in Copenhagen were invited to breakfast by the citizens of Copenhagen, and regarded with great interest by the young ladies of the town. After 1864 the street urchins cocked their thumb at them. Contemporary caricature.

gods. The question was whether the nation had enough spiritual strength to be able to grow as a result of the disaster and whether he as a poet could contribute to this.

He himself found inspiration in Italy. More than thirty years later he recalled how 'the beauty of the south, a peculiar light haze which shone like white marble suddenly revealed itself to me and set its mark on the whole of my subsequent production, even if not everything in it was beautiful'. In his now total opposition to Scandinavian romanticism, Ibsen found the people of the south also superior in moral strength: the willingness of the Italians to sacrifice everything in the battle for national unity was in shining contrast to the wretchedness at home. And down there he could really let himself go. He found an outlet not only for his anger, but also for his need for liberating, lively social contact. The very distance from his home country gave him a freedom and a courage he had never before felt, while at the same time his thoughts and longings constantly returned there: 'To the huts of the snow-land / from the wooded shores of the south / there rides a horseman / each night that falls' (Burnt Ships).

The art of the south moved him deeply. Not the master-pieces of antiquity, for in those he missed 'the expression of the individual and personal', but gothic architecture and baroque sculpture, which impressed him profoundly. Ibsen did not become 'a bit of a classicist' as Bjørnson had hoped, but on the contrary was strengthened in his urge to break all æsthetic conventions and go his own way.

He even abandoned the æsthetic attitude. As he wrote to Bjørnson in the autumn of 1865, 'the chief result of my stay abroad (...) lies in my having purged myself of the æsthetic point of view – which isolates one and makes one demand to count for something in oneself. Æstheticism in this sense now seems to me as great a curse to poetry as theology is to religion'. He added that Bjørnson had never been burdened with this kind of æstheticism and makes use of a phrase from 'On the Heights': 'You have never gone and looked at things through your hollowed hand'.

In this letter he also tells how he has found the form for his new drama and how work on it is progressing as never before.

Brand

Ibsen himself relates that it was after the battle of Dybbøl that *Brand* began to 'grow inside me like a foetus'. Some months later he set to work on a long poem, which later editors have called 'The Epic Brand'. It was probably conceived as a Norwegian counterpart to *Adam Homo*, a grand epic-satirical poem by Fr. Paludan-Müller, the Danish poet whom Ibsen in many ways most resembled. But progress was slow. He had followed the clergyman Koll, later Brand, to a point which corresponds to the beginning of Act II in the

16   The cathedral in Milan. As Ibsen wrote to Bjørnson in
1864 – 'any man who could conceive the plan for such a
work, could hit on the idea of creating a moon in his spare
time and throwing it up into the heavens'. Baroque sculpture
and gothic architecture were those aspects of Italian art which
made the deepest impression on Ibsen.

play, when in St Peter's one summer day, 'a strong, clear
form' for what he had to say, suddenly came to him. He
began all over again, and in less than three months had
written *Brand – A Dramatic Poem*. It was published on 15
March 1866.

There is altogether far more grandeur in the dramatic
version than in the epic draft. The contemporary polemic and
satire is pushed into the background and made subordinate to
a more fundamental squaring of accounts with the nation and
the age. But above all, the main character has acquired far
greater stature and more vigorous life. In the draft he meets

an opponent of equal strength in the painter Einar: 'each strove in his own way towards God, – / one with his palette, the other from the pulpit'. But in the play, Brand is the towering loner. Without the mediation of a narrator we get close to him. Also what he preaches has acquired greater weight as well as greater sublimity. It is freed from the strict rhyme and verse form, and iambic pentameter has been replaced by trochaic and iambic tetrameters which give his passionate eloquence and pithy aphorisms far greater force.

As in the majority of dramatic poems, the main character dominates the stage from beginning to end. The others can influence him, challenge him and act as a foil for him, but only one person, Agnes, is on the same level as he, and only in one act, the fourth, does she oppose him in open conflict. Apart from that, as Ibsen wrote of Bjørnson's *Sigurd Slembe*, 'the conflict is not so much in the events as in the hero's spiritual struggles with himself, and the work may all the more be called a grand monologue as the main character is throughout presented as someone isolated in the world, as one who in a terrible sense is alone in the midst of the crowd'. This characterization fits Brand even better than it fits Sigurd Slembe.

No Ibsen hero is conscious of a higher calling than Brand, and none serves so stern a god – an Old Testament Jehovah, but 'young as Hercules'. In the name of this god he wants to restore mankind, 'so the Lord again / will recognize his man, his greatest work,/ Adam his heir, young and strong'. And it is in the name of this god that he from the beginning makes iron-hard demands of others, but above all of himself: wholeness, consistency, the will to choose, sacrifice, the giving of one's life when the calling demands it. He refuses to help the common people who are starving, because hunger is to raise them up and make them nobler; but he braves the storm in an open boat to help a soul in need.

17 Henrik Ibsen phot-
ographed in Rome
1866, the year *Brand*
was published.

He is of farming stock, but trained as a priest, and it is
out in the world that he wants to wage his war. But the
district and his family impose an obligation on him. The dark
and narrow fjord district has set its stamp on the very roots
of his being: 'There, among the beach's stones / my childish
soul learnt what it was to be alone'. And now that he has
come back, the people need him as their pastor. Agnes, who
has chosen to follow him, and has been moved by the strength
of his personality, turns his gaze 'inwards', from 'the great
open spaces' to 'his own heart'. And immediately after, he
comes face to face with his 'family inheritance and debt' – in
the shape of his mother, who for land and wealth sold her
love, and thereby her soul. The meeting is decisive. The son
takes on himself his mother's spiritual debt: 'the image of
God, which you have defiled,/ shall in me be restored, washed
clean by the will'. It is here on 'home ground' that the
battle is to be fought, 'closed in by the half-light of the cleft',
but under the banner of 'all or nothing'.

The decisive tests in Brand's life all arise out of his relation to family and district. But their intense seriousness comes from the fact that ultimately they are all concerned with the salvation of the soul. When his mother is on her deathbed, he forces himself to stay away because she is clinging to the wealth which she bought with her soul. And no sooner has she breathed her last than he is faced with the problem of Alf, the son of Agnes and Brand: if they remain in the district Alf will die, but if they leave, the forces of evil will be let loose among the people, and everything Brand has worked for will be wasted. With open eyes he chooses to stay. But not even Agnes can live here, and in the harrowing and moving scene at the end of Act IV, she confronts him with the ultimate consequences of his own work: through the super-human sacrifice which he has demanded of her – that she give up everything that reminds her of the boy – she has fought her way to a liberation which can now be fulfilled only if he lets her die.

The motifs of family and fate are intertwined with that of the gypsy girl Gerd in an ambiguous way. Brand too stands between two contrasting women characters, though here the conflict has no erotic implications. Gerd is 'a broken soul' and a sort of indirect halfsister to Brand. She too – in her own distorted way – makes absolute demands and hunts 'the hawk' as he hunts 'the spirit of compromise'. She is the first person in the district whom he meets, it is she who forces him to sacrifice his son, and it is her mother (or sister?) who compels him to demand the last agonizing sacrifice of Agnes.

In his struggle to waken both the people and the individual to personal seriousness about life, Brand meets resistance from the officials in various walks of life, who want to keep the common people in a state of immaturity and dependence. In the third and fourth acts he comes into violent conflict with the mayor – a national-romantic phrasemonger and cunning political opportunist rolled into one – and in the

18 *Brand* was published in March 1866, and in the same October Act IV was performed at the Christiania Theatre. The work was not performed in its entirety, however, until 1885 when it was staged by The New Theatre Stockholm. The illustration is from the first complete performance in Norway, the Norwegian National Theatre production in 1904. It shows Brand (Egil Eide), Brand's mother and Agnes (Aagot Didriksen) in the second act. The play was directed by Bjørn Bjørnson.

fifth with the dean who represents the insipid state church Christianity-for-everyone. With the inheritance from his mother Brand has built a new and bigger church. But before the consecration the dean suggests that Brand should moderate his demands on the individual and yield to custom and the needs of the state. At that Brand stops short; he sees that not even this church can contain his vision of the sanctified life of the individual. Only 'the great church of life' can do that. He gathers the common people round him for a revivalist procession which is to cover the whole country. But the people soon become tired, and as the only incentive

19   Brand has lost, the officials have succeeded in turning the mood against him. From a performance at The People's Theatre in 1954 with Per Sunderland in the title role (extreme right). The stage set is highly stylized in contrast to earlier performances.

he can offer them is ever more sacrifice, the officials manage to turn the mood against him. The officials also have material wealth to announce: herring in the fjord! Brand has lost. As he drags himself on alone, he sees terrifying visions of a totally materialistic, capitalist-industrialist future – a grim contrast to his earlier visions – when life in the mines and lust for money will cripple the people spiritually and morally.

In the end everything is focussed on Brand himself. Up on the mountain plateau, where we met him in the first act, he is put to the final and ultimate test. 'The Invisible Choir' tempts him to give up his struggle for the ideal, and a figure with Agnes' voice promises that everything will be given back to him if only he will let go his 'all or nothing'. Brand stands firm: 'willingly and with open eyes' he is ready to live through everything again. He also resists the temptation when Gerd tries to worship him as the saviour. But when he sees that they are standing in the Ice Church, then his longing for light, sun, gentleness and mercy break through, and his tears have a redemptive effect. He is 'serene, radiant and as if rejuvenated':

> It was an icy route that led through the law, –
> But then from above came summer sun!
> Until this day I tried to be
> A tablet on which God could write; –
> But from today the poem of my life
> Shall flow warm and rich.
> The crust is breaking.
> I can weep, I can kneel, – I can pray!

Now at last Gerd manages to take aim at the hawk, but the shot loosens an avalanche over them. Brand dies with the burning question on his lips:

> Answer me God, in the jaws of death; –
> Does not the will of man
> Count one jot towards salvation?

A voice answers: 'He is the God of Love!'

The whole work must be interpreted in the light of the final scene and this answer, but over no other detail in Nordic literature has there been so much dispute. 'He is the God of Love!' Do those words contain a judgement on Brand? Has he erred and not known 'the God of Love', only the Old Testament Jehovah? Has he himself been without love and even sacrificed those closest to him for the sake of a misunderstood vocation? Many have interpreted 'the voice' that way, and have linked its reply to something said by the wise and humane doctor in the third act. He admits that Brand has sufficient of the will of man, but his 'love account' is a blank page. In line with this, people have seen Agnes as the bearer of the gospel of love, and as the positive counterpart to Brand, and have interpreted his spiritual sibling relationship to Gerd as evidence of his mental sickness.

Others, however, have pointed to the fact that Brand calls

his god 'all-loving', but not feeble and easy-going in his love, and that Agnes speaks warmly of Brand's love not only to her but to the boy and all who seek his help. 'Oh, what a wealth of love in his strong, manly breast!' Even when he is most ruthless in his demands, it is out of love, and to save souls from being lost. Agnes is certainly of a gentler nature, and may sometimes even doubt his teaching, but in all decisions she follows him – indeed, at the critical turning points it is she who points the way. Finally one may recall Brand's own words in Act III:

> Should the will succeed in such a battle,
> Then is the time for love.
> Then like a white dove it will descend,
> Bearing the olive-branch of life.

These words correspond exactly with what Brand, in the moment of his breakthrough, says about the icy road first, and after that the summer sun. Now at last the time has come for divine love, and precisely because the will has won its victory and his soul has been 'faithful to the end'. In line with Kierkegaard's idea, mercy is the answer to the utmost effort and recognition of one's own inadequacy. But in his faithfulness Brand has gone beyond human limitations and considerations. Therefore he must die. Not even he can tear himself free from the human condition and the great web of guilt and fate: 'Condemned to death is every son of man / for mankind's sins!' But there is a tragic greatness in his attempt and in his will to perfection.

Brand is quite definitely a drama of ideas – a 'syllogism', as Ibsen himself called it. It pursues one idea, that of a calling, to its uttermost and most merciless extreme. There are many elements which are best interpreted symbolically, and indeed it would be *possible* to read the whole work as an allegorical poem, where the people of the district represent the nation, and the clergyman the poet and taskmaster. Because of the nature of the poem we have to accept that certain obvious solutions – such as sending the son away instead of letting him die – do not apply in the world of the poem. But the central characters are not mere abstractions. They are living, suffering people. And they are drawn with deep understanding and great skill. Brand is one of the sharpest profiles in world literature, but he also has an inner life which moves and appals one. However unyielding he may be in his behaviour, there are still moments when he reveals that he is vulnerable and longs for tenderness, and that he suffers immeasurably in the decisions he has to make. Against him stands Agnes, warm and loving and with a more complex nature. She sees the greatness in his words and deeds, but she also knows doubt. She is weighed down by foreboding, crushed by sorrow, humble and defenceless, impotent in her revolt, and yet she has an inner strength which carries her through everything and finally breaks out into a radiant certainty. Gerd is also a fascinating figure, distraught and visionary, frightening and mysterious – boldly realistic and at the same time symbolic.

The dramatic structure is monumental. The action is set in a mountain landscape in west Norway, as towering and dark as the main character himself. Each act builds up to a decisive choice and there is a marked rise in intensity from act to act, with a dramatic climax at the end of the fourth and a new one at the end of the fifth. The fourth act, with its spiritual struggle between Agnes and Brand and its profound reversal at the end, is one of the most powerful that Ibsen ever created. The beginning of Act V, dominated as it is by the caricatures of government officials and by the polemical sections, can seem like an anticlimax, but it sets Brand's struggle in a wider social context and highlights the final climax.

As a dramatic poem and as a drama to be read, *Brand* has

20 In 1973 for the first time The Norwegian Theatre produced *Brand* in New Norwegian – translated by Bjørn Endreson. Here one sees Liv Ullmann and Svein Erik Brodal as Agnes and Brand.

its roots in a tradition, which though it goes back to the romantic era, was still living, not least in Danish literature. Both in verse form and contemporary criticism it has affinity with Paludan-Müller's eschatological poem *Ahasuerus* (1854). But the strongest literary influences came from quite another source, namely the Bible, which was the only book Ibsen read while he was working on *Brand* – 'it is powerful and strong' – and then it was the Old Testament in particular which left its mark on his manner of expression, on the allusions, and above all on Brand's concept of God.

The link with Kierkegaard is immediately obvious. Even if Ibsen said that he had read little by him and understood even less, his thoughts were very much in the air. Furthermore both the men whom Ibsen himself mentions as models for Brand were strongly influenced by Kierkegaard. They were

the clergyman G. A. Lammers from Skien, who in 1856 had
left the state church and founded his own religious community, and Christopher Bruun, who in 1864 had gone to
Denmark as a volunteer, and who later spent much time with
Ibsen in Rome. Ibsen himself saw that there were many
points of resemblance between Brand and Kierkegaard: 'the
fact is that the portrayal of a life which has as its sole aim the
realization of an idea, will always coincide with Kierkegaard's in some respects.'

Behind the concrete resemblances there are common
historical assumptions. Both Kierkegaard's preaching and
Ibsen's Brand are offshoots of an idealistic individualism
which was a strong element in the cultural life of the period.
In the demands it makes on the individual's striving for
perfection, and in its uncomprising antimaterialism, it rises
way above all secular considerations and dismisses any
solution at a social and economic level. As Pavel Fraenkel
has pointed out, Brand is thus also in line with the 'titanism'
which characterized European cultural life from the
romantic period to Nietzsche. He may not rebel against
God like the typical titanic figures, but he creates his God
in the way he feels he, and in his opinion the times, need him:

> I must see him great and strong,
> divinely great, – for thus the age demands,
> precisely because it itself is small.

But if in its idealism the work is closely related to romaticism,
with its ethic of the will it opposes that æstheticism which is
also part of romanticism (cf. 'On the Heights'). In many
ways the uncompromising demands for truth point towards
realism, as do the portrayal of Brand's mother, and the
attacks on the official class. With its emphasis on the problems
of choice and will, *Brand* deserves a place among the classics
of existentialism.

Brand made an enormous impact on the public of the day.

Within the first year it had appeared in four editions, together totalling about 5,000 copies, and it was discussed most heatedly. Both those for and against the work regarded Brand as the spokesman of its central idea. Bjørnson raged 'against the confusion, against the abstraction which shatters all humanity. I hate the book!' Vinje made fun of the Ibsenian 'Brandianism'. Monrad had strong objections, but praised the 'grandeur of the structure' and the 'total significance', while the Danish critic Clemens Petersen found it too abstract, but wrote with insight about the development of its ideas. Georg Brandes, who was still under the influence of Heiberg, had æsthetic objections, but admitted that reading it had given him 'a profound, indeed overwhelming, impression of having stood face to face with an outraged genius, under whose penetrating gaze weakness was forced to look down'. Twenty years later Strindberg called it 'the voice of a Savonarola in the middle of our æsthetic age'. It has also been experienced as a source of ethical strength by generation after generation in all the Nordic countries, both by the young radicals of the 1870s and 1880s, and by Norwegian prisoners during World War II, as well as by countless others.

Although the work was written as a drama to be read, the writer for the theatre had not repressed himself in it. This became evident when the work was performed in the theatre, in Stockholm in 1885, in Copenhagen in 1898, and in Christiania in 1904 and many times since.

Peer Gynt

Brand was the great breakthrough for Ibsen. At a stroke it placed him among the foremost writers in Scandinavia; it won him an author's salary and gave him economic security, and it also strengthened his self-confidence and his consciousness of being called to 'that life's task which seems to me the most imperative and necessary in Norway, that of awakening

21   The first performance of *Peer Gynt* took place at the Christiania Theatre on 24 February 1876. This drawing from *Ny illustreret Tidende* of the same year depicts scenes from the play; Solveig and Peer in the yard at Heggstad, Peer and Anitra in the desert, the meeting with the Button Moulder. Mother Åse on the roof of the grinding mill, Peer at sea, in the hall of the Troll King, his dream of Solveig, and his homecoming. At the première Henrik Klausen played Peer, Sofie Parelius Mother Åse, Thora Neelson Solveig and Johannes Brun the Troll King.

the nation and urging it to think great thoughts'. That is a royal thought as bold as Håkon's!

Ibsen's position and the conditions of his life were radically altered, and he showed it by changing his appearance, and even his handwriting. In the space of an unbelievably short time, the bohemian became a man of the world, well dressed, correct, reserved, often brusque, and once in a while genial – the Ibsen we know from the majority of pictures and memoirs.

But in his writing he let himself go as never before. *Peer Gynt* is 'wild and shapeless and written with abandon' in a

22   Henrik Klausen and Sofie Parelius as Peer Gynt and Mother Åse in the first production at the Christiania Theatre in 1876. At Ibsen's request Grieg had composed music for the play, which Ibsen had originally conceived as a reading drama. The performance lasted from seven to quarter to midnight, even though the fourth act had been dropped!

way he dared to write only when he was far from home, as he himself admitted in a letter five years later: 'for you see, it was written in the summer of 1867 during my stay on Ischia and Sorrento'.

He took the material where he found it, and used it as it suited him. Peer took his name and some of his most important characteristics from the hunter Peer Gynt in Asbjørnson's tale, 'The Reindeer Hunt in Rondane'. 'He was a real spinner of yarns and a teller of tall stories who would have given you a great deal of fun. He always claimed to have been involved in those stories which other people said had happened long ago.' Out of him, Ibsen created the most versatile and vital of all his characters, and made him the hero of a new and remarkable folktale. Other motifs and characters followed – the ride on the buck, the *sæter* girls, Gudbrand Glesne, Bøygen and the Devil in the nut – while for his part Ibsen created characters who could just as well be part of folktale or legend — the Troll King, the Button Moulder, the Lean One. His language and style are also more uninhibited than ever before – at least since 'The Mountain Bird'. The text abounds in Norwegian dialect words, inflections and phrases, and the whole style has a country flavour which admirably suits the subject.

In short Ibsen, more than anyone else before him, had drawn on national-romantic sources, which here for the first time really come into their own in an innovatory work. And at the same time, the poem turns out to be, besides much else, a major confrontation with that very same national romanticism.

What *Peer Gynt* directly or indirectly owes to other works of literature has been discussed by many. Certain features of the

23 Bjørn Bjørnson as Peer Gynt in the Christiania Theatre production in 1892. On that occasion, as several times later, only the first three acts were performed.

24   Peer and Mother Åse during a performance at the Christiania Theatre in 1892. Bjørn Bjørnson as Peer and Sofie Parelius as Åse.

plot resemble Ibsen's own *Olaf Liljekrans*, and a couple of details come from the legends he had collected in 1862. Fairy-tale plays, such as *Vinægers Fjeldeventyr* (*Vinægers Mountain Tale*) By Wergeland and *Huldrebryllupet* (*The Hulder's*[1] *Wedding*) by Botten Hansen, H. C. Andersen's fairytale 'Elverhøi', Welhaven's ballad about Eivind Bolt, J. L. Heiberg's 'apocalyptic comedy' *En Sjæl efter Døden* (*A Soul after Death*) and Bjørnson's *Synnøve Solbakken*, have all left identifiable marks. The genre of the work is related to Goethe's *Faust* and Oehlenschläger's *Aladdin*, while Peer has many of the same weaknesses and shares something of the same fate as the title figure in Paludan-Müller's great verse

[1] In Norwegian folktales the *hulder* is a beautiful and alluring woman, but unfortunately she has a cow's tail. Tr.

narrative, *Adam Homo*. For once Ibsen has not tried to cover his tracks, but lets Peer throw out quotations – more or less distorted – mainly from Holberg, but also from the Bible, Shakespeare. Molière and Goethe.

But Ibsen picked and chose and reworked. He also did this with the models and contemporary material he used. To be sure, a number of allusions and satirical thrusts have a reference which today can be found only in learned commentaries, but they count for little in the whole context of the work, the teeming, rich play about Peer Gynt.

Like *Brand, Peer Gynt* is a dramatic poem in five acts, but whereas the dramatic structure in *Brand* is taut and linear, in *Peer Gynt* it is rich and varied. In the original, the greater part of the poem is written in simple, free *knittelvers*, a four-stress line with rhyming couplets, and the versifier in Ibsen has made superb use of the freedom which the form allows. But he has also used a great many other metres to make a varied combination, and many important sections – such as the ride on the buck, 'one castle built on another', Åse's death and the clergyman's funeral speech – stand out on account of their distinctive metric character. And even when he uses a trochaic tetrameter, the 'heaviest' metre in *Brand*, it here acquires a lighter character and a quicker pace because of the vocabulary and sentence structure used.

There are even greater differences between the two poems in landscape background, plot framework, time span and scenic development. From beginning to end *Brand* takes place in a narrow and dark fjord in western Norway, and in the nearby steep mountains, and the action is limited to five years. *Peer Gynt* spreads itself broadly both in time and space, begins in a light and open valley in eastern Norway, continues on wide mountain plateaus, takes us to Africa's sunny shores and then back across the sea again. The setting is constantly changing, and more than one scene has obviously been included as a 'caprice', a whim, as Ibsen himself said about the scene with the Strange Passenger.

Nor has he taken the dividing lines between the genres too seriously. Long, narrative and pure fantasy sections are inserted, such as the buck ride, Åse's death and the clergyman's speech – the latter depicting a whole life in epic form. Indeed the whole work romps from genre to genre – fairytale play, rural sketch, character tragedy, fantasy satire,

25 & 26   This and the following illustration show scenes from *Peer Gynt* in the Norwegian National Theatre production in 1902. Both pictures show the emphasis that was placed on sets. The illustration above shows Peer (Halfdan Christensen) talking to the captain of the ship crossing the North Sea (Act V, Scene 1). In the picture on the next page Peer has found his way back to Solveig (Aagot Kavli, later Nissen) and asks her to proclaim his sins. But Solveig replies, 'you made of my life a beautiful song./ Bless you for coming at last!/ And blessed be our meeting this Whitsun morn!' This colourful production was shown one hundred times.

Aristophanic comedy, dream play and morality, the old play about Everyman. And above all it has a multitude of characters and a range of moods and registers which are without parallel in Norwegian literature.

In *Brand* everything takes place on the same level of reality – The Invisible Choir and The Figure in the last act clearly being visions or hallucinations. In *Peer Gynt*, on the other hand, fantasy and reality constantly merge. Figures from one suddenly appear in the other. Indeed, secret thoughts and desires can step suddenly forward as actualized facts, and in parts of the work, particularly in the last act, 'inner' and 'outer' worlds simply cannot be separated – the landscape in which Peer finds himself is co-extensive with his own mind.

If at first sight the work appears wild and chaotic, it nevertheless has a pattern and order of its own. The distance between acts and scenes can be enormous as far as time and place, character and mood are concerned, but parallels, contrasts, contrast similarities and echo effects of many kinds tie them all together. For example, threads run from the courtyard of Heggstad in the first act, via the hall of the Troll King in the second, through the cosmopolitan 'chorus' round Peer's 'altar to the golden calf', and the scene with the Arabian chieftain and Anitra, to the battle with the apes and the crowning of the emperor in the madhouse – all in the fourth act. And the fifth act as a whole, which is also linked to the first and second, is a counterpart to the third. In the fifth act Peer is on his way back to the world he once left, his real 'empire', and the contrast effect is emphasized in the many details, recognitions and memories that emerge.

The inner unity is also reflected in recurring motifs, such as the emperor and princess dreams, key words, and groups of symbols which weave in and out through greater and lesser parts of the work in a rich and meaningful harmony and counterpoint. Among these symbol clusters are the widespread animal symbols which, as Harald Noreng has pointed out, correspond to the sensual and animal element in Peer, in sharp contrast to the religious and virginal attributes which are associated with Solveig. Another group of symbols develops out of the buck ride, which we hear about in the first act. It crops up again in many other forms, but is always associated with dreams and the flight from reality. A third cluster runs from the ruined family home, through dreams of rebuilding it and fantasies about castles, to Solveig's hut – the only real bit of work Peer ever does – and the ultimate goal of all Peer's wanderings.

And what about Peer himself? Does he hold together as a character? The question has often been asked, and with good reason, for is there any connection between the imaginative young lad of the first three acts, the cynical speculator, tycoon and opportunist of the fourth, and the old man who fights his way towards redemption at the end? Are they not at least three different characters?

It goes without saying that Peer is a complex figure, and to a large extent the work is about his lack of character, his adaptability and his role-playing – in other words, precisely about his lack of identity and inner coherence. When in his old age he peels the onion, he never finds the core, and he has to face the fact that he has never been himself. However, there is cohesion.

The young Peer is full of possibilities. The strongest and most striking talent he has is his imagination, which shows itself in his dreams and visions. But it is also his most dangerous temptation, because it lures him away from reality and offers him the easiest way out, so that his will never get a chance to grow strong. It becomes part of his nature to go 'round about'. But imagination is also linked to that which is most sensitive and good in him. It is that which enables him to *see* Solveig. It is related to his longing for purity. And it is a combination of these things which makes him flee from Solveig after his meeting with the Woman in Green in the third act – the decisive turning point of his life. In the same way it is tenderness, and a delight in fantasy as well as cowardice which inspires the last fairytale he makes up for his mother, and which helps her through the last moments of her life, even though it perhaps also leads her soul astray. It is his final outstanding achievement as a poet, an equivocal gesture of thanks to her who first taught him to avoid things difficult and unpleasant by taking flight in imagination.

From the beginning Peer has dreamt of power and greatness and an empire, and in the fourth act he is well on the way to achieving them. Free from any scruples, he has exploited the possibilities which the international market has offered, and he has faithfully followed the motto which the trolls taught him: 'To your own self be – all-sufficient!' He has also

27 The best known *Peer Gynt* production from the inter-war years was the one put on by the Norwegian National Theatre in 1936, with Halfdan Christensen as director. The illustration shows a scene between Alfred Maurstad as Peer and Johanne Dybwad as Mother Åse. Oliver Neerland had painted the sets.

28   In 1948 *Peer Gynt*, translated into New Norwegian by
Henrik Rytter – was produced at The Norwegian Theatre by
Hans Jacob Nilsen, and with music by Harald Sæverud. It was
played as an 'anti-romantic work'. This scene is typical: Peer
(Hans Jacob Nilsen) sits with his back to the dying Mother
Åse (Ragnhild Hald) as indicated in the text. This was in
contrast to traditional performances in which Peer sat on the
edge of the bed and supported his mother.

used his imagination, but only for the purpose of speculation,
or when other ambitious projects have been the object, such
as his plans for Gyntiana or Peeropolis. Perhaps the memory
of Solveig does live on in a corner of his mind – if it is not just
the reader who is given a glimpse of her, as an ironic
commentary on Peer's devaluation of women. He has at any
rate developed his ability never to commit himself, and to go
'round about', to the point of virtuosity, so in the end he is
crowned emperor, 'emperor of the self' – in a madhouse.

In the fifth act it is not because Peer has become a
different person, nor because he has grown old and wants
to reform, that he is gradually compelled to take stock of his

life. It is because the wreck, the Strange Passenger, the clergyman's speech and the auction of the family farm gradually awaken 'the reality of dread' in him. It is because a distant glimpse of Solveig in the fourth act makes him dimly perceive what he has squandered, and because the Button Moulder and the threat of the button mould awaken his naked instinct for self-preservation. That, at least, has always been strong in him. And it is not fear of punishment for sin, but the fear of coming to an end, and of the accusation that he has never in fact been himself, that drives him from defence to defence, until he is eventually forced to admit that the accusation was true: 'They can write above it: "Here No One lies buried".'

Here at last Peer has reached rock bottom. But it is precisely now that he is ready to meet Solveig. She says that in one place he has been himself, 'in my faith, in my hope, and in my love'. At last he has found his way home. And Solveig sings him to rest, 'Sleep and dream, my precious boy!'

Even this ending has been understood and evaluated in different ways. The majority agree that in his meeting with Solveig, Peer finds himself again, and is thus saved, or *perhaps* saved. But after that the paths diverge. Some believe that it is Solveig's love which redeems him, but, like Vinje, have found such an interpretation irrational and even offensive. Others have accepted such an ending but have interpreted it religiously: Solveig is a holy virgin who atones for Peer's wrongdoing and intercedes for him; she saves him in the same way that Beatrice saves Dante, Gretchen Faust, and Alma Adam Homo.

The objection to this view is that throughout the work the demand has never been for specifically Christian values, but for the identity and integrity of the personality, and that for Peer the problem has been one of avoiding the button mould, not of being saved in the traditionally Christian

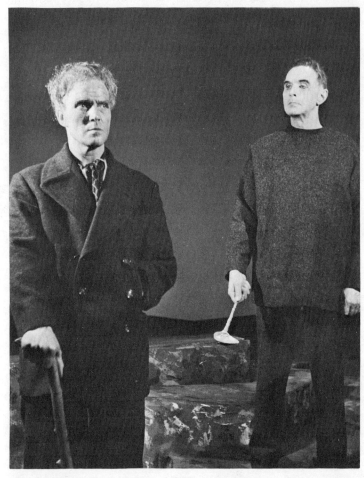

29 Peer as an old man (Rolf Søder) meets the Button Moulder (Johan Norlund) in Act V. From The Norwegian Theatre production in 1962.

meaning of the word. Furthermore one can recall the Button Moulder's words in the middle of Solveig's song, 'We will meet again at the last crossroad, Peer / and then we'll have to see; I say no more'. This could mean that Peer still has time and that nothing is settled yet. In that case the writer has placed the ultimate end outside the drama, and left it to the readers themselves. Many years earlier he had praised Andreas Munch for doing just that in *Lord William Russell*, and this practice was soon to become a common feature in Ibsen's plays.

The greatest contrast between Ibsen's two great dramatic poems lies in the main characters themselves. Over and against the unyielding ascetic and ethical Brand with his incorruptible will to meet the demands of reality, there stands Peer the sensualist and fantast who lacks will and the ability to take a stand. Both are seen in the light of an idealistic, religiously determined concept of personality, for the demand is to be, or become, 'oneself' as one 'sprang created from the mind of God' – 'with the stamp of destiny on one's brow'.

Judged by such standards, Peer falls far short; he has always been 'sufficient unto himself', but precisely because of that never 'himself'. Despite this the poet has not been able to suppress his sympathy for the dreamer, the compulsive liar, the fantast and charmer. He has left him with one final chance, just as he could not give up all hope for his own people either.

With *Peer Gynt* as with *Brand*, the poet wanted to teach the nation to think 'great thoughts', but this time he used the negative method. Looked at from a socio-historical point of view Peer is a period type, an expression of the first stages in the breakdown of the rural community – the farmer's son who abandons farm and property, makes his way in the world as a speculator, but who goes under morally. However, he is also a national character type, the Norwegian per-

30   Part of Alf Rolfsen's *Peer Gynt* fresco (1967) in the Hansa Hall, Bergen. This section shows the young Peer in the power of his dreams and visions.

sonified so to speak, so this work too can be read as an allegory about the Norwegian people. The satire is directed against the national romantic glorification of the past, and against self-righteousness and the flight from reality and responsibility into fairytales and noncommittal dreams of renaissance and future greatness. And it extends to a reckoning with the cultivation of the life of the imagination, the child of good fortune, and 'the gifted idler', elements which all belong to the romantic tradition: behind Peer we glimpse Askeladden and Aladdin. But most of us have also felt the truth of the words spoken by the Man in Grey, 'the blood is never so thin,/ that we don't all know we're akin to Peer Gynt'.

Ibsen's contemporaries set the work far lower than succeeding generations have done. Many were offended by the satire and the book did not sell well. Of the reviewers, Bjørnson was fairly positive, 'it is not a coherent, rounded poem (...) but a spirited and daring fancy in which the brilliant pattern of intertwining thoughts is not always successfully transformed into flesh and blood', but 'it is a piece of tidying up done with a strong tool'. Brandes maintained that the work was neither true nor beautiful, and that 'scorn for humanity and self-hate (...) were a bad foundation on which to build a poetic work'. But he praised the versification, and later he developed a quite different view of the work. Clemens Petersen wrote that neither *Brand* nor *Peer Gynt* were poetry because 'the ideal is lacking', and that Ibsen had less of a feel for 'the life of reality' than for 'the laws of reality'.

It was about Petersen's judgement that Ibsen wrote to Bjørnson in indignant fury and said, 'my book *is* poetry; and if it is not, it will become so. In our country, in Norway, the concept "poetry" will one day take its shape from my book'. In this he was to be proved right. To the publisher he wrote that people had found more satire in the work than he had intended, 'Why can't people read the book as a poem, for it was as such that I wrote it'. On this point also, posterity has agreed with him. Attention has been directed more and more to the human content and to the poetic richness of the work, to the problem of personality and identity, to the variety and many layers of meaning, to the imaginative flight and lyricism, to the unparalleled technical skill, the subtle patterns and connections, the humour, the intuitive understanding and the wide applicability of the satire. It is these characteristics which have won a universal response for

Ibsen's most Norwegian work, and have made it one of his main contributions to world literature.

In 1876, long before *Brand*, *Peer Gynt* was produced on the stage of Christiania Theatre. Edvard Grieg had written music for it, but the text had been considerably shortened, and among other things the entire fourth act had been removed. In this way the whole production acquired a lyrical-romantic character, which later productions emphasized even more – occasionally too the fifth act was dropped. The play that was to be a showdown with national romanticism had become a national festival production. In 1948, however, Hans Jacob Nilsen broke with this tradition, interpreted the play as an 'anti-romantic' work, as the literary historians had done, and thereby opened a new chapter in the stage history of the work.

A light-hearted interlude

With *The League of Youth*, written in Dresden during the winter of 1868–69, Ibsen again produced something new, a prose comedy in a contemporary setting. As so often before, Bjørnson had beaten him to it, on this occasion with a play called *De Nygifte* (*The Newly-Married Couple*). Common ancestors to both were French dramatists such as Scribe, Augier, and Dumas the Younger. But Ibsen went further than all of them. Whereas all the characters in *The Newly-Married Couple* speak in very much the same way, in Ibsen's play we hear for the first time on stage, a Norwegian prose dialogue in which each character is allowed to speak in his own distinctive way – from Stensgård's empty rhetorical tirades to Daniel Heire's needle-sharp sarcastic remarks. And Ibsen's admiration of Holberg has given the play such a richness and cheerful liveliness that Bjørnson's little homily is quite put in the shade. There are echoes of the French dramatists both in the plot and in the characterization of certain types, but in contrast to them Ibsen has given his milieu strong local – from the Skien of his childhood – and his characters are a product of Norwegian reality rather than of foreign literature.

He found his material in the political life of the day, for it was just at this time that Søren Jaabæk, the leader of the farmers in the opposition, and Johan Sverdrup, the leader of the liberal intellectuals, were uniting their forces. Furthermore, there can be no doubt that Bjørnson himself, as well as other politicians on the left, lent traits to the phrasemonger and opportunist Stensgård, and that Ueland, Jaabæk's predecessor as the farmers' leader, is echoed in the wily old *Stortings* member Lundestad. But Stensgård is also related to Peer Gynt: it has been said that he is Peer Gynt as a politician.

The lawyer Stensgård wants a political career, wants to become an elector, a member of the *Storting*, and eventually a cabinet minister, and with these aims in mind he needs both allies and a wealthy wife. He sweeps the young people along with him on his flow of empty words, proposes right, left and centre, woos the rival bigwigs of the place, and tries to make use of a promissory note which he gets hold of. But he is outwitted, gets caught in his own trap, and in the end achieves nothing but to be thoroughly exposed. The plot is complicated, but elegant, and in the true spirit of comedy. All the characters, from Stensgård to Bastian Monsen, Madam Rundholmen, the printer Aslaksen, and the experienced, malicious and scandal-mongering Daniel Heire are drawn with great satirical skill.

But in the midst of all his opportunistic striving Stensgård does have certain redeeming features. Basically he is a man of good faith, full of naive confidence in himself and Our Lord – indeed, in this he to some extent resembles Håkon in *The Pretenders*. And the author's mouthpiece, Dr Fjeldbo, gives a psychological explanation for his weaknesses, ascribing his unintegrated personality to an unhappy home and an unfortunate upbringing. There is also an element of social criticism in the play. The chamberlain represents an old patriarchal aristocracy, in contrast to the landowner Monsen, who stands for the bourgeois upstarts and capitalists of the new period. They have bitter truths to tell each other. The chamberlain points to Monsen's dishonest speculation, while the landowner reminds him that he is the son of a log-driver who worked himself to death in the chamberlain's forests: 'have you even once experienced what those who work for you must put up with in the forests and down along the river, while you sit in your cosy sitting-room and reap the fruits? Can you blame a man like that for wanting to work his way up?'

The most obvious indicator of things to come in Ibsen's writing, is the young Mrs Selma's revolt against her husband and her father, who have both treated her like a doll, and have never allowed her to share their troubles. As Kristian Elster and Georg Brandes pointed out at the time, there was material here for a whole play. Ten years later Ibsen wrote *A Doll's House*.

To his publisher he wrote saying that *The League of Youth* was 'the most artistically polished' work he had ever pro-duced. To Brandes he emphasized that he had achieved 'a strong realistic colour', and that among other things he had managed 'the feat' of getting by without the aid of a single monologue or aside.

The models, however, were furious, and at the Christiania Theatre young radicals, led by Olaus Fjørtoft, greeted the play with jeers. Kristian Elster attacked the work as a 'piece of party propaganda' and maintained that bias had got the better of the artist in the portrayal of Stensgård. Jonas Lie thought the satire was 'disgusting', criticized the caricaturing of living models and asserted that the entire play was built on 'unpoetic philistinism'. The conservatives on the other hand cashed in on the play and regarded Ibsen as their man.

The really explosive element was still safely hidden.

Ibsen was becoming a recognized writer. In the summer of 1869 he was given a grant to study art and literature in Sweden. There he participated in the great nordic conference on orthography, and King Charles XV gave him his first medal, which to his unfeigned delight was soon followed by others. The king also saw to it that Ibsen was allowed to represent Norway at the opening of the Suez Canal that autumn. A year later he wrote that this had been 'the most interesting and instructive period of my life'. The most immediate literary impact of these experiences is evident in a long historical-philosophical poem, 'Balloon Letter to a Swedish Lady', which had contemporary relevance, and which he wrote the following year. Less obvious, but hardly less important is the significance these events had for a world-historical drama, which had long been in his mind.

'– in the chains of verse'

Ibsen had written poetry before he wrote plays, and for a long time he continued to write lyric poetry on the side. While he was employed at the theatres in Bergen and Christiania he produced much occasional verse, prologues, salutatory poems, wedding songs and such like. In the lyric form more than in drama he could also give direct expression to what was stirring in him, and his most significant poetry tended to come from crisis periods in his life.

Many of the poems had been printed in newspapers and periodicals, but Ibsen had several times thought of publishing a collection, and in 1870, shortly after Bjørnson's *Digte og sange* (*Poems and Songs*) had appeared, he set to work, gathered together all his poems, threw out a large number – among them the majority of occasional poems – reworked the remainder, and finally published the collection under the title *Digte* (*Poems*) in 1871.

As he wrote in a letter to Brandes shortly after, 'there are

31   Henrik Ibsen photo-
graphed in Copenhagen
during the summer of
1870. Georg Brandes,
who met him for the first
time the following year,
said of him, 'I found him
handsome. He had a
magnificent forehead,
bright eyes, and long,
wavy hair.'

things both old and new in it, and there is much which I do
not consider to be of any great importance, nevertheless it is
all part of my development'. Despite this he was not content
to leave the poems as they were, milestones in his development. The main line in the collection is certainly chrono-
logical, but there are many departures from this, and he
altered many of the older poems so that they corresponded
more to his attitudes and artistic standards as they were in
1871 than to those of the period when they were first
conceived.

Some of the poems, such as 'My Young Wine', 'The Gully',
'In the Gallery' and 'A Swan', build freely on motifs from
the poetry of his youth. Others, such as 'Fiddlers' and
'Afraid of the Light', are extracts from older poems or
cycles of poems, and both these and the majority of others

from the 1850s are shortened and condensed. At the same time the vocabulary has been given greater character, a more specifically Norwegian colour, and greater power of expression and imagery. The last two stanzas of 'Building Plans' – which, incidentally, was cut from four to three stanzas – are a good example of these changes. The 1853 version (printed 1858):

> I built a dream castle. It went easily and fast.
> I set myself two goals, one little and one great.
> The great was to become a man immortal,
> The little to own a lovely lily flower.
>
> To me there seemed a glorious harmony in the plan
> But afterwards disturbances have come.
> As I acquired discretion, the whole thing seemed quite
>   mad,
> The great became so little, the little to me was all.

In *Poems*:

> I will build me a cloud castle. Two wings shall shape it
>   forth;
> A great one and a small one. It shall shine across the North.
> The greater shall shelter a singer immortal;
> The smaller to a maiden shall open its portal.
>
> A noble symmetry methought shewed in my double wing;
> But afterward there came a sad confusion in the thing.
> The castle went crazy, as the master found his wits:
> The great wing grew too little, and the small one fell to bits.

In the penultimate stanza direct speech replaces report, concrete images abstract concepts, and precise and special words vaguer ones; everything is now linked to the castle. And if we compare the last two lines, it becomes apparent that the poem has acquired a totally new meaning: the poet's ambition has placed love completely in the shade.

Just as significant is the alteration to the last stanza of 'The Miner', which was made, characteristically enough, in the difficult period after *Love's Comedy*. In the first version from 1850, the stanza begins thus:

> So it goes blow on blow
> Till he sinks, tired and weary –

In the version from 1863 and in *Poems* we read:

> Hammerblow on hammerblow
> Until life's last day.

The continuation is almost as before:

> No ray of morning shines.
> Nor dawns the sun of hope (in 1850: clarity).

But through the change the meaning and the attitude have become different – hopelessness has given place to an indomitable will and sense of vocation. But the most important change occurs in the third stanza. In 1863, as approximately in 1850, it reads, 'Break me a way, heavy hammer,/ to the chamber of nature's heart! – –' But in *Poems* we read, 'Break me a way, heavy hammer,/ to the heart-chamber of what is hidden! –' The poet is speaking through the miner and he has a different goal; now it is the human mind and the laws of life, not the mysteries of nature, of which he wants to get to the heart.

Changes such as these bear witness to Ibsen's personal and artistic growth. They also say something about his aims as a lyric poet, and reflect a clear shift away from late romantic imitation and towards a more concrete and 'realistic' mode of expression.

The poems range from songs to narrative poems, from occasional to deeply personal verse, from lighthearted poems and mischievous anecdotes to chiselled poems of ideas, remonstrance and confrontation with the times. Form and tone vary with subject and attitude, but all the same there are strong common elements, namely terseness, concentration, a highly condensed intellectual content and highlighting. The words are few and simple but highly charged, and nouns and verbs tend to stand alone without adjectives or adverbs. The sentences are also simple, but often constructed or combined so as to form antitheses or paradoxes: 'Tears play in his laughter,/ the lip speaks when it is silent' ('On the Heights').

Simplicity and concentrated force also characterize Ibsen's use of images. These are few, but well chosen. He prefers to hold on to one image, one concrete situation or one idea throughout a whole poem, and to exploit it to the utmost. This can result in a consistent allegory, as in 'Building Plans'; or in profound symbolism as in 'With a Waterlily', 'The Miner' and 'On the Heights'; or in an expressive illustration to a line of thought as in the references to the Egyptian remains in 'Balloon Letter to a Swedish Lady' or in a lyrical connecting motif, like the sailing boats in Øresund in 'Rhymed Letter to Fru Heiberg'.

The concentration of vocabulary and imagery is supported and reinforced by Ibsen's versification. The verses (lines) are usually short, rarely more than four beats, and often only two. The rhythm is usually strong, the rhymes heavily stressed, and important words tend to be in rhyming positions. All this contributes to giving couplets, stanzas and poems a pointed, epigrammatic character which is peculiar to Ibsen.

In contrast to Bjørnson he has a clear and characteristic preference for certain stanza forms. Far more often than is usual among lyric poets, he uses the simplest of all, rhyming couplets, perhaps in order to give the words a sarcastic twist as in 'The Ground of Faith', or challenging emphasis, 'You deluge the world to its highwater mark,/ and it will be my pleasure to torpedo the ark' ('To my Friend the Revolutionary Orator').

However, he could also use more distinctive forms. In many of his best known poems the stanzas consist of nine lines with the rhyme sequence **a,b,a,b,c,d,c,c,d**. This form is presumably Ibsen's own discovery, and it occurs in descriptive and narrative poems, including 'On the Heights' and 'Terje Vigen', but mainly in polemical poems of confrontation, such as 'A Brother in Need' and 'The Murder of Abraham Lincoln'. With its stark form, its consistently monosyllabic rhymes and the interjected penultimate line which postpones the ending and heightens the expectation, 'the Ibsen stanza' acquires unique intensity and power of expression. As Hallvard Lie says in *Norsk Verslære* (*Norwegian Versification*), it seems to be the ideal form of expression for the two sides of Ibsen's poetic talent as it 'gives ample space both for objective epic-dramatic presentation and for subjective pathos' – and, one might add, for biting scorn too.

With forgotten promises, with betrayed words,
with the torn paper of treaties,
with the breaking this year of your oath from the past,
thus have you fertilized history's field.
And yet you expected, happy of mind,
an autumn of the very best kind!
Look now, your seed grows. What a brilliant sight!
You stare, you cannot make it out –
for in place of corn, daggers are growing!

The antitheses and contrasts of individual lines, couplets and sentences correspond to the more extensive conflicts and inner tensions of the poems as a whole. These tensions can be of many kinds, idea and reality, depth and surface, great and small, past and present, true and false, dream and deed, courage and cowardice, mountain and valley, even 'Field Flowers and Potplants'. And nearly always it is the con-

frontation of opposites that is the point of a poem. At the
the end the tension may be resolved, unresolved or left
ambiguous; there may be a sudden reversal, a threatening
warning or a bold paradox; or the whole poem may be
ambivalent or culminate in an ironic twist, for in Ibsen's
poetry the dramatist is also very much in evidence.

It is in the poems of Ibsen's youth that one finds most
lyrical feeling. These may express fear, poetic dreams, doubt
and sorrow, impotence and defiance, as in 'Fiddlers', 'Bird
and Birdcatcher', 'Afraid of the Light', or they may be the
product of a lively historical sense, as in 'In Akershus' or a
youthful romance, as in the poems to Rikke Holst (see p. 34).
Lyrical harmony and intimacy also characterize a number of
songs from the plays, such as 'Now wall and roof are one',
from *The Pretenders* and 'Agnes, my sweet butterfly' from
Brand. But the finest and most delicate of all Ibsen's lyric verse
is a little poem from his time in Rome, the brilliantly concentrated 'Gone', which is full to the brim of the poetry of the
inexpressible:

> The last guests   Now in tenfold desolation
> we followed to the gate: lay house and garden
> the last words of   where so recently
>   farewell   sweet music had charmed me.
> the nightbreeze stole.

> It was only a dance
> before the dark night;
> she was only a guest, –
> and now she has gone.

The great majority of Ibsen's poems are reflective, the
intellectual content counting for more than the mood, and
situation and imagery being used primarily to express or
illustrate the idea. The various scenes of 'On the Heights'
illustrate conflicts of values and ideas, and even the mag-

32   Ibsen had wanted to be a painter, and continued to draw and paint right up to the beginning of the 1860s. Altogether extant are more than sixty original works by him – including costumes and sets. This painting – from the Grimstad period – of 'Elijah under the broom in the desert', is the only known painting by Ibsen with a religious motif.

nificent verse narrative about Terje Vigen is something of a philosophical poem. Typical are a number of short poems in which one single image or a simple chain of events have an unexpressed or understood allegorical content. Examples of this are 'Complications', which resembles Heine in its wit, and a number of miniature poems which presumably concern the poet himself, like 'The Power of Memory'.

In his many poems of political and moral confrontation and social criticism, Ibsen speaks without a disguise and we can follow a clear line of development. The poems which are inspired by 'the breach of promise to Denmark' are carried along by moral indignation, but do not, however,

33 Johanne Luise Heiberg (1812–90) entered the ballet school of the Royal Theatre in Copenhagen when she was eight years old. When at the age of sixteen, she became an actress at the royal court, J. L. Heiberg, who was later to become her husband, had already written several vaudevilles for her. By Easter 1871 when Ibsen wrote his 'Rhymed Letter to Fru Heiberg', she had retired from the stage, having played more than 270 roles.

have reference beyond Scandinavia. In 'The Murder of Abraham Lincoln' the indignation is just as strong, but the perspective is international and the basic thought historical-philosophical, a sort of moral 'disaster theory',

Just let 'the system' be turned right around;
and the sooner revenge will come and pass sentence
on the last day of the lie of the times!

The perspective is even wider in 'Balloon Letter to a Swedish

Lady', which was inspired by Ibsen's journey to Egypt and
the Franco-German war. But here the poet is more of a
spectator waiting to see the outcome. He sets the lifeless
Egyptian gods and the full-blooded, human Graeco-Roman
ones up against each other, and sees parallels between the
dead 'kingdom of the Pharaohs' and the new militaristic
Germany. Against the mechanized mass apparatus he sets up
the living individual, against military discipline the longing
of the period for art and beauty. And from 'the token
victory' of the moment, he looks forward to other times – 'on
a voyage to the land of promise'.

The newest of the longer poems in the collection, 'Rhymed
Letter to Fru Heiberg', stands in a class of its own. The
flight of the imagination is freer, and the verse form – a richly
varied 'Wergeland's trochee' – is much lighter than elsewhere
in Ibsen's poetry. Furthermore the choice of images has a
playful charm which admirably suits the subject, the actor's
art, the most fleeting of all arts – 'a child of fragrance,/ of
inspiration,/ of a mood,/ of an individual, of imagination'.

In this poem he can still say with full justification,

> Prose style is for ideas,
>   verse for visions.
> The mind's delight and mental woe,
> the griefs which on my head fall like snow,
>   and the anger which flashes,
> to these I give life most freely
> when in the chains of verse I write.

All the same Ibsen did not write many more poems. The
most important were a monumental, forward-looking and
personally coloured poem for the thousandth anniversary of
the unification of Norway (see p. 103), and a 'Rhymed
Letter to Georg Brandes' (see p. 110), both of which were
included in later editions of *Poems*. But he soon gave up
writing verse altogether, presumably because he could no

longer reconcile the art of verse with his growing demand for realism. He even declared that verse was a dying art form, and attached all the more importance to 'the incomparably more difficult art of writing honest, straightforward, everyday language', as he put it in 1883.

Emperor and Galilean – 'my masterpiece'

In the summer of 1871, Ibsen wrote to his publisher, 'this book will be my masterpiece, and it is absorbing all my thoughts and all my time. Here the critics will find the positive philosophy of life which they have been demanding of me for so long'.

'This book' – a play about Julian 'the Apostate' – had been on Ibsen's mind since his first summer in Rome. Other

34   Emperor Julian 'the Apostate' (331–63), Roman emperor from 361. Marble statue in the Capitol Museum, Rome. It took Ibsen nine years to complete *Emperor and Galilean*, his ten act drama about the seeker Julian. Afterwards he always regarded it as his main work.

topics and plans had intervened, but now that *Poems* was out of the way, he set to in earnest, and in the autumn of 1873 *Emperor and Galilean – A world-historical drama*, was to be found in the bookshops. It is in two parts, each containing five acts: *Cæsar's Apostasy* and *Emperor Julian*.

As Ibsen himself pointed out, the form of the play most resembles that of *The Pretenders*; it is in prose, there are great jumps in time and place, many changes of scene, rich background scenes and a large gallery of characters. But it stays even closer to its sources: the Roman historian Ammianus Marcellinus first and foremost, then several newer studies and dissertations (mainly German), and finally a series of articles published in the Danish newspaper *Fædrelandet* in 1866. In essentials the outer action follows the historical accounts closely, and even though Ibsen has taken many liberties concerning character portrayal, background description and manner of expression, these too are based on the sources; indeed, many lines are taken straight out of letters which are quoted there. As Ibsen wrote to the English critic and translator Edmund Gosse, he had wanted to give the work 'the most realistic form'. The reader should have the impression that what he read really had happened, and therefore he did not use verse; 'my new play is not a tragedy in the ancient sense; what I have wanted to describe is people, and it is precisely for that reason that I have not let them speak in "the language of the gods" '. And to Brandes he wrote, 'what the book is or is not I do not care to investigate; I only know that I have received a powerful impression of a fragment of human history, and what I have seen, that I have tried to reproduce'. All the same the work is something far more than an accurate and colourful presentation of a remote period. It is in the profoundest sense a world-historical drama, an historical-philosophical play of ideas from a critical period of struggle, and with implications far beyond it, a work of literature about the aim and

purpose of history, about freedom and necessity, and furthermore one of the most penetrating psychological studies Ibsen
had ever done. Rooted though the characterization and
central intellectual conflicts may be in the sources, in the
inner drama, the poet goes far beyond them.

Throughout the entire work Julian stands alone at the
centre. In *Cæsar's Apostasy*, which spans a period of ten years,
we follow him through a turbulent and painful process of
maturation. He is a young man with great talents, and an
honest Christian among all the hypocrites and court serpents
'of the emperor's own faith' in Constantinople. But as a
possible successor to the throne he has since childhood
lived in constant dread of being cleared out of the way, and
this fear has left deep marks on him. He is therefore all the
more interested in what Libanius relates about the free and
happy life at the Academy in Athens, and when in a vision
he learns that he has been chosen to take up the struggle with
the pagan philosophers on their own ground and with their
own weapons, he feels it as both a liberation and a vocation,
and sets out with a good will.

Because he always demands harmony between life and
teaching, he becomes just as disappointed with 'the friends
of wisdom' in Athens as he was before with the Christians.
The old heathen beauty lures and fascinates him. But he
learns one thing in Athens, 'the old beauty is no longer
beautiful, and the new truth is no longer true'. He therefore
yearns passionately for a new revelation and goes to the
mystic Maximus in Ephesus, where during occult ceremonies
he is again elected: he is to 'establish the kingdom', and he
is to do it 'by the way of freedom' which is also 'the way of
necessity', by willing that which he *must* will. Maximus
initiates him into the doctrine of the three kingdoms:

First there is that kingdom which was founded on the tree
of knowledge; then that kingdom which was founded on

the tree of the cross -. (...) The third kingdom is the great mysterious kingdom which shall be founded on the tree of knowledge and the tree of the cross together, because it hates and loves them both, and because it drinks of living springs under Adam's grove and under Golgotha.

In a mystical seance, Maximus lets him meet two of 'the three great helpers in denial', Cain and Judas. The signs point to Julian himself as the third. He tries to tear himself free, 'I defy necessity! I will not serve it. I am free, free, free!' Precisely at that moment the message arrives that he has been appointed Cæsar, heir presumptive to the emperor, and he takes the announcement as confirmation that he has been called. But in his new position he determines to continue to be what he always has been, 'the poor lover of wisdom'.

From now on, external events play a greater part. The emperor's intrigues, his wife Helen's sensuality and falseness behind a mask of piety, and the grandiose hypocrisy of the priests round her coffin – all these things drive Julian to a confrontation, and strengthen his hatred for Christ who, with the emperor, had made his youth one continuous nightmare: 'oh, he is terrible, this mysterious ... this merciless god-man!' Everywhere Julian turns he is faced by His 'pitiless demands':

> When my soul curled up inside me, in gnawing and consuming hatred for my family's murderer, then the commandment said: 'Love thine enemy!' When my spirit, bewitched by beauty, thirsted for the customs and images of the ancient world of the Greeks, then the Christian commandment stopped me with its, 'Seek only the one thing needful!' When I felt the sweet longings and desires of the flesh for this or that, then the Prince of Self-denial would terrify me with his, 'Die unto this world, that you may live in the one hereafter!'

Furthermore, everything human has become forbidden since

'the seer from Galilee began to rule the world': to live has
become to die, and to hate or love has become a sin:

> Every healthy fibre of our souls rebels against it! – and
> yet we are to *will* against our own wills! We must, must,
> must! (...) It is more than a doctrine that He has spread
> throughout the world: it is witchcraft which takes hold of
> the minds of men. He who has once been under his spell,
> – I do not think he can ever tear himself totally free. (...)
> We are like vines transplanted in a foreign soil; – if you
> moved us back, we would die, but we do not thrive in the
> new soil.

Much of the play is concentrated into this outburst: Julian's
most hidden motives, his desire for freedom and his impotence, much of the experience he has already gained, and
much that he is to learn later. However, the first part ends
with a scene of high drama in which, goaded by Maximus,
he tears himself free from the 'Galilean' and leads a rebellion
in order to become emperor himself.

Emperor Julian is about the attempt to 'establish the
kingdom'. As soon as he assumes power, Julian begins his
task of realizing his dream. He is high-minded to all except
flatterers and informers and he proclaims total liberty of
conscience. He himself worships the old Greek gods. But it
soon becomes clear that the old beauty *is* dead. His own
relation to the gods is dead, characterized by learning, not by
faith, and the Dionysian procession which he leads fills him
with disgust: 'what has become of beauty? Will it not rise
again at the Emperor's bidding?' However, all attempts are
vain. Maximus asks how he knows 'That the beauty of
ancient times was beautiful – in itself – and not just in the
imagination of the beholder?' Julian has to concede this to
him; men no longer see with the same eyes as before; the
'Galilean' has transformed them.

From the beginning it is the Christians who are the greatest problem for the Emperor. When he learns that they have attacked heathen temples he reacts brutally. But he succeeds only in strengthening them, in frightening away the luke-warm, and in sparking off in the believers the desire for self-sacrifice. The Apollonian procession in honour of joy and beauty meets a procession of Christian prisoners on the way to their death, but full of an ecstatic belief in the efficacy of martyrdom. The two processions confront each other and the opposing spiritual forces are expressed in a kind of antiphon. Julian is soon compelled to recognize that the 'Galilean' is alive, 'however much both Jews and Romans imagined that they had killed Him; – He lives in the stubbornness in the hearts of men, in their defiance and scorn of all visible power'. Indeed, when Julian becomes so fanatical, it is really because in his innermost heart he is fighting against the power which 'the Prince of Self-denial' has over him. As the Christian Macrina puts it later, 'what is it that you hate and persecute? It is not Him, but your belief in Him. And is He not just as alive in your hatred and persecution as He is in our love?'

Maximus, who once forced him to choose between 'Galilean' and 'Emperor' now rebukes him for the battle he has waged against Christ, for both Emperor and Galilean shall be superseded by him who is to come, but not perish, just as the child is superseded, but continues to live in the youth, and the youth in the man. Julian has wanted to turn the youth into a child again and to stop him from becoming a man. By doing that he has also drawn his sword against 'that which is to be, – against the third kingdom where the two in one shall rule', he who can assimilate both 'the kingdom of the flesh' and 'the kingdom of the spirit', but go beyond them both: 'Emperor-God, – God-Emperor. Emperor in the kingdom of the spirit – and God in that of the flesh. (...) Logos in Pan – Pan in Logos'.

Julian recognizes his defeat, and now turns against his external enemies with even greater zeal, throwing himself into battle against the Persians in order to subjugate the world. The questioning idealist and high-minded ruler reveals his other side. Fear makes him morbidly suspicious, dreams nourish his megalomania and vanity, and his thoughts of liberation end in empty talk about the books he is going to write, while his faith in divine signs and portents becomes impotent dependence on soothsayers and oracles. In adversity he fluctuates between overconfidence and a desperate desire for destruction. And his grudge against the 'Galilean' becomes even more bitter because he, the Emperor, stands alone and deserted, while the carpenter's son 'sits as the king of love in warm, believing human hearts'. It is not until he is mortally wounded that Julian regains something of his former self: he speaks of death and of his own fate as a pupil of Socrates, and in his very last words all his longing for beauty and his dreams of the sun flare up again '(...) Beautiful garlanded youths ... dancing girls ... but so far away./ Beautiful earth ... beautiful earthly life .../ Oh sun, sun, why didst thou deceive me?'

Maximus admits that he was misled by signs that spoke with double tongues when in Julian he 'glimpsed the reconciler of the two kingdoms'. But 'the third kingdom shall come. The spirit of man shall reclaim its heritage – and then incense will be burned for you and your two guests in the symposium'. The Christian, Basil, sees in Julian, 'a glorious shattered instrument of the Lord, (...) a rod of chastisement – not for death, but for resurrection'. 'Terrible is the mystery of election', exclaims the devout Macrina; but 'if you were *forced* to err, then it will certainly be counted to you as righteousness on that great day when the Mighty One shall come in a cloud to judge the living and the dead and the living dead! –' Both for those who see the victory of Christianity as the ultimate goal, and for him who believes

35   The first Norwegian performance of *Emperor and Galilean* took place at the Norwegian National Theatre in March 1903, thirty years after its publication, with Egil Eide playing the part of Julian. Only the first part, *Cæsar's Apostasy*, was shown. The very first performance took place in Leipzig in December 1896.

that the road to the third kingdom leads *through* Christianity,
Julian, as a 'sacrificial offering to necessity' has served a
higher goal, the purposive development of the universe.

Emperor and Galilean was conceived and written as a drama
to be read. It is weighed down by its philosophical content
and its wealth of realistic details, and is little suited to the
stage. Even as a reading drama it can be tedious in parts.
Despite this, the first part, *Cæsar's Apostasy*, is a powerful work,
carried by Julian's restless quest, his fear and his longing, his
rebellion and impotence, and the sudden breakthrough of
will and energy. Each act concentrates on one phase in
Julian's life, and leads by an inner necessity into the next,
until the whole play culminates in the great scene of dis-
ruption at the end. The second part, *Emperor Julian*, has a far
looser structure. It is true that the time span is much shorter,
only one and a half years, but the course of events is
broken into small scenes, many of which do little more than
report on events which have happened elsewhere. Here too
there are powerful and compelling scenes – such as the
meeting between the procession of prisoners and the Apollonian procession in Act II – and many substantial exchanges. But the interest fades. This is both because from the
start Julian's struggle is so clearly doomed to fail, and because
in the last acts the struggle takes place almost exclusively on
the outer plane. However, it is also because as Emperor, and
particularly as military commander, Julian has lost most of
the questing urge which motivated him in the first part, and
soon sinks to become a half laughable, half sinister caricature
of himself. Whereas in the first part he is made more noble
than the histories portray him, towards the end of the second
he is made more repellent than he appears even in contemporary Christian chronicles. It is not until the very last
scenes that he regains his original stature, and the end is
gripping.

While working on the play, Ibsen wrote to Gosse saying, 'it is part of my own spiritual life that I am setting down in this book. What I describe I have lived through myself in different forms; and the chosen historical theme has a much closer connection with the movements of our own day, than one would at first imagine'.

Ibsen had always followed the events of his times closely. The February Revolution had provided inspiration for his first play, and the Danish-Prussian War had done the same for *Brand* and *Peer Gynt*. In a similar way the major events of the period round 1870 formed the background to his *magnum opus*. These were primarily the Franco-Prussian War, the establishment of the Commune in Paris, and the *Kulturkampf* between Bismarck and the German Catholics. Ibsen believed that both politically and culturally a new era was just round the corner. In his own thinking too a great shift was taking place.

The revolutionary and anarchistic moods that pervade the poems 'The Murder of Abraham Lincoln' and 'To My Friend the Revolutionary Orator' now break through with violence. In a letter to Georg Brandes in December 1870, he says that he is not interested in 'special revolutions, external revolutions, political revolutions etc.'; what is needed is a 'revolution of the human spirit'. And some months later, 'the state must be abolished. In such a revolution I will take part'. In its place he wishes to establish 'voluntary participation and spiritual kinship as the only essentials for union – there you would have the beginnings of a freedom which would really be worth something'. Greater things than the state – 'all religion' – will collapse, and he adds that neither moral concepts nor the forms of art have eternal validity. Shortly after he complains that the Paris Commune has 'spoiled my beautiful state theory – or to be more precise, my non-state theory'.

He can, however, also assert an opposing point of view.

He admires the unifiers Cavour and Bismarck; they have written 'the law of the times', the law of unification, which Scandinavia also ought to adopt ('Celebration for the One Thousandth Anniversary'). In letters he occasionally rages over the 'inner dissolution' which Jaabæk and Sverdrup are blamed for (see p. 81). He even thinks the Norwegian conservative government is far too lenient, because 'people who let Jaabæk and Bjørnson remain at large, deserve themselves to be put in chains'. He maintains that intellectual liberty thrives best under a despotism, for it is the struggle for liberty that he is concerned about, not liberty itself.

In a similar manner Ibsen can hold conflicting views of history. In 'Balloon Letter to a Swedish Lady' he trusts optimistically in the fact that 'the march of mankind' is 'constant' and 'always rising'. But it also happens that world history can seem to him 'like a single great shipwreck', as he says in a letter to Brandes in September 1871.

Two months later Brandes began his revolutionary lectures about main currents in nineteenth-century literature. The following spring the first series, *Emigrantlitteraturen*, appeared in book form. As Ibsen wrote, 'no more dangerous book could fall into the hands of a pregnant writer. It is one of those books which set a yawning gulf between yesterday and today'. He is not sure that the 'spiritual constitution' of the Scandinavian countries is strong enough to take it – 'but that is not the point; whatever cannot tolerate the ideas of the age, must fall'. Nor does he know what the result will be of 'this fight to the death between two epochs ...; but anything is better than the existing state of affairs; that is the decisive thing for me'. He adds that he does not expect any permanent improvement from the victory, for 'all development up to now has been nothing more than a stumbling from one mistake into another. But the struggle is good, healthy, invigorating'.

A struggle between two epochs as one phase in a never

ending historical process – that was what he saw in Julian's time too. And in one central area the similarity is even more striking: then as in Ibsen's day Christianity and humanism faced each other in irreconcilable conflict, though now it was Christianity that was losing ground to a new humanism. In the play Ibsen tries to give history a meaning beyond all errors by fastening his hope on 'that which is to be'. 'The third kingdom' represents a synthesis of irreconcilable opposites, not a compromise, but a higher unity which subsumes and supersedes them both.

As the two Norwegian scholars Halvdan Koht, and more particularly Paulus Svendsen, have shown, this doctrine has its roots in an old and strong European tradition, which can be traced back to neo-Platonism. Later writers such as Schiller and Heine, Wergeland (see p. 12), the Swedish poet, novelist and thinker, Viktor Rydberg, and the philosopher Hegel had imagined a synthesis of Christianity and humanism, spirit and senses in a happier future. Ibsen could have received inspiration from several of them, though particularly perhaps from Hegel. *Emperor and Galilean*'s close affinity to the Hegelian way of thought is also revealed in the basically dialectic philosophy of the work, though it was Ibsen himself who formulated the doctrine of 'the third kingdom'. Even though the sources contain some support both for the doctrine and the part it played in the history of Julian, the ideas are in the main free creations, coloured by Ibsen's own experience of the time in which he lived and by his struggle for a new 'world view'.

As far back as his time in Grimstad, Ibsen had called himself an atheist, but works such as *Lady Inger*, *The Pretenders*, *Brand* and *Peer Gynt* all bear the indelible stamp of Christian dualism. Even if Brand in his church speech dreams of a harmonious union of flesh and spirit, his whole character is strong evidence to the power which 'the Prince of Self-denial' had over the writer. He later tried to distance himself from Brand's religious preaching. In 1870 he maintained that the poem was a totally æsthetic work, that it was a matter of indifference to him what it had built up or torn down, and that in it he had freed himself from something which he was inwardly finished with. Having so passionately fought the 'æsthetic' in himself he could then give free rein to the imagination in *Peer Gynt*, and in 'Balloon Letter' describe the Greek gods' sensuous life of beauty and happiness.

Against this background it is easy to understand what Ibsen is referring to when, in a letter, he writes that 'in the character of Julian, as in the greater part of what I have written in my mature years, there is much more that I have spiritually lived through than I care to account for to the public'. The conflicts between Christian demands and the desire for freedom, asceticism and a longing for beauty, fear of life and dreams of happiness had deep roots in him. That is also why the dream of a higher unity became a vital necessity for him. But there is also personal experience behind Julian's words about one who has once been under the sway of the Prince of Self-denial – 'I do not think that he can ever tear himself totally free' and this was to become evident time and again in Ibsen's writing.

The problem of fate, the relation between 'freedom' and 'necessity' in Julian's life, is something Ibsen too had grappled with, and the idea of vocation had always had a special place in his work; since the hero's vocation was at one with the divine will, betrayal of it was an irreparable sin. In the course of working on Julian, however, Ibsen had 'in a certain way become a fatalist'. The influence of Hegel's philosophy of history had presumably contributed to this, as had probably also Arthur Schopenhauer's ideas of a 'world will', which had recently gained new currency through Ed. v. Hartmann's work, *Die Philosophie des Unbewussten*. In the Hegelian system, all wills are forced to serve universal reason; in Schopenhauer and Hartmann they (the wills) are, without knowing it, tools of the metaphysical will. In none of them is there any place for individual free will, and for that reason there is also no conflict about a person's calling: freedom is necessity: to will is to have to will. In Hegel's dialectic, denial and one-sidedness are necessary elements in the overall pattern, the unfolding of universal reason through opposites. Likewise also in Ibsen's drama: it is Julian's tragedy that he errs, but it is a necessary erring which serves a higher purpose, and for this reason 'the sacrifice to necessity' may be seen in a redeeming light.

There are obvious similarities between the historical roles of Skule and Julian, as Ibsen sees them, but at the same time there is a major difference: as long as Skule fights against Håkon, he is also opposing God's will, whereas Julian serves the universal will by and through his denial. Skule has much of Ibsen the doubter in him, Julian something of the Ibsen who, for the sake of the future, is willing to place 'a torpedo under the ark'.

Emperor and Galilean was received with friendly interest by critics and public alike, and the first edition was soon sold out. Brandes, in *Det nittende Aarhundrede*, asserted that 'it is full of superb things, very profound, very poetic', and the young Arne Garborg wrote a complete short monograph on the play. However, it is probably one of the least read of Ibsen's works. Both parts received their first performance in Leipzig in 1896, and in Oslo sixty years later, on both occasions in drastically shortened versions. Ibsen regarded the drama, and continued to regard it, as his main work, and for anyone who wishes to familiarize himself with Ibsen's intellectual world, it is one which cannot be ignored. The belief that here he had formulated his 'view of life' was something he reaffirmed in a speech as late as 1887. For him the natural scientific law of evolution is valid for 'the spiritual factors of life' also, and he continues:

36   In 1956 the Norwegian National Theatre staged *Emperor and Galilean* in a version adapted for the theatre by Irene Bille Ibsen, and produced by Knut Hergel. The illustration shows a scene between the young Julian (Knut Wigert) and Helen (Wenche Foss).

I think the time is imminent when political and social concepts will cease to exist in their present forms, and that out of them there will emerge a unity which, for the time being, will carry within itself the conditions for human happiness. (...) I believe that poetry, philosophy and religion will merge into a new category and into a new life force, of which those of us who are now living can have no clear conception.

On various occasions people have said of me that I am a pessimist. And indeed I am, insofar as I do not believe in the eternal validity of human ideals.

But I am also an optimist insofar as I fully and confidently believe in the ability of ideals to propagate themselves, and in their evolutionary capability.

To be more specific, I believe that the ideals of our age, while they are disintegrating, are tending towards that which in my drama *Emperor and Galilean* I have called 'the third kingdom'.

He did not always express such confidence, but again and again we catch a glimpse of the dream from *Emperor and Galilean* in and behind the plays which followed.

The tragedy about Julian marks a watershed in Ibsen's authorship. Up till then he had seen his characters and themes in a romantic-idealistic and Christian-Platonic perspective. The basic contrast had been between idea and reality, and spirit and nature in the individual. From now on the conflict is between the individual and existing social barriers, between, on the one hand, the dream of a truer, freer and happier human existence, and on the other, all the dead weight of the past in society and the human mind. And this battle is fought out here and now. *Emperor and Galilean* was Ibsen's last historical drama, and in many ways it provides the background for his socially critical and psychologically analytical contemporary plays. It was the first work in which he set absolute realism as his goal. In this too it marks the transition to the next phase of his authorship.

Society on the stage

Ibsen and Brandes – and 'a corpse in the cargo'

There are good reasons why, in the years of ferment surrounding *Emperor and Galilean*, Ibsen should have chosen Georg Brandes to whom to express himself so openly. For several years he and Brandes had followed each other's activity with growing interest and sympathy. In 1867 Brandes had written an essay about Ibsen in *Dansk Maaneds-skrift*, which was critical of much in his writing, but full of admiration for the personality behind the works. This was the first lengthy discussion of Ibsen, and it contributed much to making him known in Denmark. Two years later they began a correspondence which came to mean a great deal to them both.

Brandes in the meantime had freed himself from Heiberg's æstheticism, with the help of the French critics, Sainte-Beuve and Taine. There is much to indicate that the impression made by Ibsen, both through his works and his personality, had contributed to this liberation. It must surely have impressed him when Ibsen wrote to him in 1869 saying, 'of course I bow to the laws of beauty, but I have no regard for its conventions' for 'even that which is formally ugly can be beautiful by virtue of its inherent truth'. And it must have made an even stronger impression when, a year later, Ibsen wrote to the young critic, 'what is needed is a revolution of the human spirit, and it is you who should lead it'. The exceedingly radical ideas which Ibsen propounded in his letters had shocked Brandes to begin with – this he reveals in letters to a friend – but they had presumably encouraged the radicalization which eventually bore fruit in *Emigrant-*

litteraturen. When that work appeared, it was Ibsen's turn to be overwhelmed (see p. 103). They met, too, and when they parted Ibsen enjoined Brandes to stir up the Danes, while he for his part would deal with the Norwegians. But they did not agree on everything. Brandes placed great emphasis on political freedom and on the battle against the church, while Ibsen made a sharp distinction between outer and inner – spiritual – freedom. Despite this they grew closer to each other, and in 'A Rhymed Letter' which was printed in the first volume of *Det nittende Aarhundrede* (1875), Ibsen openly takes up a position beside Brandes.

The poem is a confrontation with the age on a grand scale: 'the ship of Europe' has set out to sea for new shores, but when the ship is half way it slows down, while despondency and fear creep up on the passengers who are dozing in the oppressive air:

> There lay a statesman who twisted his mouth
> as for a smile, which ended in a gape;
> a learned professor rolled over on his side,
> at odds, so it seemed with his own knowledge;
> a theologian pulled a blanket up over his head;
> while another dug it down in his pillow, –

and 'halfway / between restless sleep and nightmare' a voice can be heard, 'I think we are sailing with a corpse in the cargo!'

'A Rhymed Letter' was a prelude to Ibsen's realistic modern dramas, and in a certain sense they all have this theme in common: the voyage to new shores, but with a corpse – be it social or individual – in the cargo. The conflict between ideal and reality, aspiration and ability has acquired a new content and a new character.

Pillars of Society

As early as 1870, the year after *The League of Youth*, Ibsen had jotted down notes for a new comedy – but one with a deeper meaning: 'there is something of significance beneath the surface; something symbolical, the liberation from all narrow conventions; a new, free and beautiful life. It is around this that the play revolves'. This play never saw the light of day, but the basic idea and many individual points were to crop up again later in *Pillars of Society*. Many other things came in between: *Poems, Emperor and Galilean*, new editions of old plays. And in the summer of 1874 Ibsen was in Norway for the first time in ten years. He was acclaimed by the conservatives, mainly for *The League of Youth*, but he was shocked by the 'narrow conventions' and the fear of new ideas, which expressed itself in, among other things, the persecution of the two feminist pioneers, Camilla Collett and Aasta Hansteen. The fear of new ideas was also evident in the university's attempt to exclude the radical historian, Ernst Sars, and in Professor Lochmann's matriculation address for that year, the notorious 'quarantine speech', in which he suggested that Norway should establish a *cordon sanitaire* against the new ideas. All this strengthened the oppositionist in Ibsen, it influenced 'A Rhymed Letter', and it drove him to take up his old plans for a comedy and to remould them. Many of the motifs from 'A Rhymed Letter' – the symbol of the ship, the unhealthy air, America as the image of a new and better world – were here to be given dramatic life.

In the spring of 1875 Bjørnson published *Redaktøren (The Editor)* and *En Fallit (A Bankruptcy)*, the first realistic modern dramas in Scandinavia, and Ibsen read them both, though particularly the second, with great interest. In the autumn he wrote to his publisher about his own new play, saying that it could be regarded as a counterpart to *The League of Youth*, and that it 'takes up several of the more significant issues of the day'. But two years were still to pass before it was finished. There are more drafts of this play than of any other play by Ibsen, and they show how he grappled with the new form, and worked his way towards a natural, everyday style of speech.

The framework of the plot is lifted straight out of Norwegian society of the period. Consul Bernick's shipyard is at the point of transition between patriarchal and larger, more industrialized and impersonal forms of production. The workers are afraid that the new machines will take away their work, and the threat of dismissal has become an instrument of power which, when he is in a tight corner, the consul uses against his trusted foreman, Aune. The conflict between workers and employers has begun to grow sharper. As Aune says at the beginning of Act I, 'My society is not the consul's society'. It is the age of the construction of the railways, and the pillars of society are buying up land which will increase in value. It is also the age of Plimsoll and his struggle to reform the shipping laws. It had become known that Norwegian as well as British shipowners were speculating and sending unseaworthy ships to sea. Bernick himself resorts to such measures, though for more special reasons. The milieu is a 'society of bachelor souls', without the least understanding of women and their position: a narrow, self-righteous and censorious small town environment, very different from the free, sunny world we sense in the distance.

Stensgård launched an attack on existing society and only made a fool of himself. Here on the contrary it is society, represented by the figure of one of its main pillars, Consul Bernick, which is exposed, thanks to the defiant intruder, Lona Hessel. In contrast to the conventions and hypocritical morality of society, 'the moral linen', she represents a broader view and a higher morality, an unconditional demand for truth from the individual. In the eyes of society, Consul Bernick is a man of honour, a benefactor towards all those who live off the activity he has set in motion. But *she* knows that the whole of his life's work has its origins in the betrayal of love and in lies, and it is chiefly out of concern for him, his inner being, that she now demands that he tell the truth. The concern for society is far less than in *A Bankruptcy*. Even so, Lona Hessel's closing maxim emphasizes that 'the spirit of truth and freedom – they are the pillars of society'.

The play fulfilled the demands which the period made of a bourgeois comedy, and it was a huge theatrical success in both the Scandinavian and German speaking countries. Compared with Ibsen's later dramas it can seem primitive, both dramatically and psychologically, but it has a large and colourful gallery of characters, with many amusing types, and instant scenic charm. It is exciting, it entertains and touches, and it ends harmoniously and happily as a comedy should.

There is, however, something strange precisely about the ending. Considering his villainy, Bernick gets off remarkably lightly. His last and worst piece of villainy, which it is true was confounded, he does not even mention in his speech to the people. He is also assured control of the properties which he has acquired at the very moment when he renounces them. Indeed, the whole 'settling of accounts' establishes his moral authority more securely than ever before. To that extent it is tempting to see the final scene as ironical, as the British Ibsen scholar J. W. MacFarlane has done – to see it as a comedy about people's capacity to be hoodwinked or about a society where 'the important people' always get things the way they want them. But this was hardly what Ibsen intended, for Lona Hessel would then have to be seen ironically too, and her actions regarded as misguided, and this would conflict both with the character portrayal and with the spirit and mood of the play. On the other hand, an ending to match Bernick's misdeeds would imply a more fundamental criticism of society than the genre could tolerate.

Even in his early preparatory notes, Ibsen described his next work as a 'modern tragedy'. It was here that he was to put a large question mark against existing society, and it was here that he was to lay the foundations of a new dramatic tradition.

A Doll's House

Since ancient times, tragedy had been associated with the world of the aristocracy, and had concerned noble individuals and great heroes. In the eighteenth century the German writer Lessing and others had written some bourgeois tragedies, but right up to Ibsen's time bourgeois characters, like farmers and workers, had figured almost exclusively in comedies and farces. In 1844 the German Friedrich Hebbel published a bourgeois tragedy, *Maria Magdalena*, of which Ibsen thought very highly. The female protagonist dies as the victim of conventional morality, but represents a higher one, and the technique is to some extent retrospective. This may have provided Ibsen with some inspiration, but, in the portrayal of women, in tragic depth and technical mastery, *A Doll's House* – written in Rome and Amalfi in 1879 and published the same year – goes far beyond Hebbel's tragedy as well as Bjørnson's *Leonarda*, which had appeared some months earlier.

There are many strong and well integrated women in Ibsen's plays, and the majority of them have 'that instinctive ability which unconsciously enables them to choose aright' (speech from 1879). However, it is only in the great dramas of ideas and in historical settings that they are able to express themselves fully. In a bourgeois society, as portrayed in *Love's Comedy*, *The League of Youth* and *Pillars of Society*, they are pushed to one side, declared incompetent, and hemmed in by customs and conventions. Rebellion smoulders in several of them, but it is not until *A Doll's House*, which is based on a contemporary marital story, that it develops into an irremediable conflict between the woman and existing society.

Outwardly Nora Helmer is the ideal wife according to the ideas of the age, a 'lark' for her husband, and a charming mother to her children. But for many years she has struggled and saved in secret in order to pay back the loan she raised to save her husband's life. The fact that she has forged a signature is something to which she never gives a thought; 'boring society' and its laws lie beyond her horizons, and with good reason. Besides, she knows that she acted out of love, and she cannot believe that the law would not take such motives into consideration. For Helmer, the competent lawyer, on the other hand, the very thought of forgery is profoundly disturbing. His moral principles coincide completely with the laws of society, and he thinks about the moral consequences. The lies with which a forger must surround himself are bound to poison the home and corrupt the children. The idea causes Nora to pale, but she tosses her head and protests for the first time, 'it is not true. Never in all eternity is that true'.

Her confidence in Helmer, however, is unshaken. When, totally unsuspecting, he says he would be man enough 'to take everything on himself', she recoils in fear, and as the moment of revelation approaches, there wells up in her an agonizing expectation of 'the miracle' – that out of love for her, Helmer will step forward and take the blame on himself. She knows that she could not accept such a sacrifice; 'the miracle' would also be 'terrible', and to prevent it from happening, to clear his name, and herself bear the consequences of what she has done, she is willing to take her own life.

Krogstad's letter forestalls her, and the revelation opens an abyss between the couple, and between reality and the illusions on which the marriage has been based.

Helmer reveals that he is far from the chivalrous knight

37   The first Norwegian performances of *A Doll's House* took place at the Christiania Theatre on 20 January 1880, with Johanne Juel as Nora. The National Theatre in Bergen had its première ten days later. This drawing by the stage decorator Olaf Jørgensen in *Ny illustreret Tidende* shows Nora in the tarantella scene in Act II of the Christiania Theatre production of 1880. Dr Rank (Hjalmar Hammer) is sitting at the piano, Mrs Linde stands speechless in the doorway, while Helmer (Arnoldus Reimers) exclaims, 'but my dear Nora, you're dancing as if your life depended on it', to which Nora replies, 'it does'.

in whom Nora has believed; he is a narrow minded bourgeois citizen, who is totally dependent on the estimation of others, and on his own position. He is just as remote from her dreams of 'the miracle', as she ultimately is from the 'lark' with whom he has played. Essentially they are strangers to each other. When Nora 'throws off her fancy-dress costume' and turns to confront Helmer, she directs a bitter indictment against her father and against him because they have treated her like a thing, a toy, a doll; but through them she also arraigns society which keeps women in a state of immaturity. It has now become necessary for her to examine those 'truths' which have been instilled into her, and to find her own: 'I must try to see who is right, society or I'.

She sees too that she has been wrong about herself as well as about Helmer, and that she has committed a crime against her own human worth in a marriage based on false premises. For this reason she has to break away and even leave her children: 'as I am now, I can be nothing for them'. A new union with Helmer would have to assume that they had both changed to such an extent that their life together would be a real marriage. This we can presumably interpret to mean a relationship without dissimulation or role playing, between equal and free individuals. But the last thing we hear is the gate slamming shut.

'The modern tragedy' does not end in ruin, as Ibsen originally had intended, but in a new start. However, values are destroyed as the whole of Nora's world collapses. This happens precisely because she is true to the best in herself. She grows in stature, and is purged by suffering. In defeat she is victorious. In the majority of theories about 'the tragic' these are significant factors. When everything lies in ruins round her, Nora emerges strong and independent as never before, and takes the consequences of her newly gained understanding; she is in the process of becoming 'herself'; at the same time she points to a freer and more honest humanity in a healthier society. It is in this sense that she is a modern, tragic heroine, and the play precisely what it claims to be, a 'modern tragedy'.

Nora has become one of the great female roles in world drama, bearing the stamp of its age, but not limited by it, typical, but also refreshingly individual. She constantly reveals new facets and fluctuates between extremes, between happiness and despair, hope and fear, love of life and longing for death, the dream of 'the miracle' and a sharp sense of reality, impotence and a calm purposefulness. Throughout all these changes, however, there is direction to her development. Right from the beginning the 'new' Nora reveals herself in glimpses, grows from scene to scene, and finally stands forth as a complete figure. It has been maintained that Helmer is not a sufficiently strong opponent for her; readers too have wondered what Nora could see in this narrow minded pillar of the community, and how she could expect the 'miracle' from someone like him. But he is able and honourable, cultured, and chivalrous too – so long as he is not put to the test. In his virtues, as in his limitations and inner poverty, he too is an expression – and a victim – of the male-dominated society: oppression recoils on the one who is placed in the role of oppressor.

Technically, Ibsen still makes use of such well worn tricks of the theatre as the impending threat, the short period of grace, the letter in the letter box. But at the same time, it is precisely here that he develops the dramatic technique which was to provide the basic structure of nearly all his contemporary plays: the *analytic* and *retrospective* technique, in which the decisive events have all taken place long before the curtain rises, but are exposed and brought to a head in the present moment. The technique was not new. Sophocles had used it, Schiller and Hebbel had revived it, in Norway Maurits Hansen had used it in many of his short stories, and even Ibsen had used it as early as in *Catiline*, and more extensively in *Lady Inger of Østråt*, *The Vikings at Helgeland* and *Pillars of Society*. But it is not until *A Doll's House* that the uncovering of the past and the true state of affairs becomes as important as in certain Greek tragedies. Basically, in *A Doll's House* everything revolves round such an exposure. The revelation takes place slowly and, in the most subtle interplay with that which is taking place in the present, it propels the action forward. At the same time, new aspects of the past action and the responses they evoke give new meaning to what happened, create new understanding, broaden the scope and open up new perspectives. The unravelling of the individual's past becomes at the same time an exposé of social injustice and social hypocrisy.

Closely associated with this technique is a stern dramatic economy. As in *Pillars of Society* the 'unity of place' is observed. The temporal framework is a little wider, a couple of days, but the dramatic action is far more concentrated. The scenic progression has acquired a strong, rhythmic forward movement, the tension rises to ever greater heights; the rhythm of the play proceeds from the intimate, realistic glimpses of everyday life and the sudden, disturbing interruptions in the first act, to the desperate tarantella at the end of the second, through the calm before the storm at the beginning of the third up to the exposure and confrontation at the end.

The gallery of characters is limited to a minimum, basically five in all; they are all necessary for the central action, and four of them act as foils for the main character. Krogstad and Mrs Linde are, each in their own way, both parallels and contrasts to Nora, and the relationship between them emerges as an illuminating contrast to Helmer's marriage. Dr Rank, who in the draft is very much a mouthpiece, not only has a realistic function, but is also responsible for creating mood and symbolic overtones; between him and Nora there exists a secret sympathy.

Here for the first time we see extensive use made in drama of what the English scholar John Northam has called 'visual suggestion'. By this is meant those visual elements on the stage which acquire a deeper, illustrative or symbolic meaning in addition to their realistic function. These may be a special feature of stage setting, or a character's dress, or movements. An example is the Christmas tree, which in the first act prepares us for a happy and cheerful family occasion, but which at the beginning of the second stands 'stripped of its decorations, tattered and with burnt-down candle stumps'. Others are Nora's game of hide-

38   The tarantella scene from a production of *A Doll's House* at the Central Theatre in Oslo in 1922, with Gyda Christensen as Nora and Theodor Berge as Helmer.

and-seek with the children in Act I, and the preparations for the fancy-dress party in Act II. Particularly significant is Nora's use of her fancy-dress costume and her everyday clothes, her colourful shawl and her black one.

A comparable dualism characterizes the dialogue. With its everyday vocabulary, interruptions, self-corrections and incomplete sentences, it comes close to colloquial speech. Even the long and weighty replies in the final confrontation scene have a familiar and natural air. Despite this, the dialogue is strictly controlled. Replies interlock; there is scarcely one which does not have a demonstrable dramatic function, and every now and again they rise above daily speech, in rhythm, syntax, vocabulary and imagery acquiring a concentrated power of expression. Often the effect is linked to key words

39   The lawyer, Krogstad (Jørn Ording) explains to Nora (Liv Strømsted Dømmersnes) that he has discovered that she has committed forgery, and he threatens that 'if I am kicked out a second time, you're going to keep me company'. From a performance of *A Doll's House* at the Norwegian National Theatre in 1957.

– 'the miracle' – and to expressions and phrases which are repeated in scene after scene. Or it may be linked to certain words or cliches which suddenly become ambiguous, as when Dr Rank thanks Nora for 'the light', or disturbing, as when Helmer says of the tarantella, 'you are dancing as if your life depended on it', and Nora replies, 'that is precisely what it does'.

In *A Doll's House* Ibsen's modern drama found its typical form, but it was Nora and her rebellion which caused the play to be a universal sensation. It was soon translated into German, Finnish, English, Polish, Russian and Italian, and it was staged in theatres as far flung as South America and Australia. The famous Eleonora Duse played the leading role in St Petersburg. It was explained and attacked in newspapers, periodicals and books; it was condemned from pulpits and discussed by lawyers – and Strindberg made brilliant fun of it in *Giftas I (Marriage I)*. What made people most angry was that Nora leaves her husband and children, and in several German theatres the final act was altered so that she chooses to stay. In order to prevent even worse falsifications, Ibsen himself prepared a draft for an ending of this kind, and permitted it to be used as 'a last resort'. Later he regretted this: 'I could almost say that it was precisely for the sake of the final scene that I wrote the whole play.' With its original ending, *A Doll's House* has reached farther into the four corners of the world than any other Ibsen play. It has revealed a strange capacity to stimulate an audience to discussion, to compel and to arouse – and this in widely differing times and places.

Ghosts

Ibsen had been living in Italy during 1878–79, and in the autumn of 1880 he settled in Rome, this time for five years. Here he started to write a short autobiography, 'From Skien to Rome', and perhaps too an outline of the play which was later to become *An Enemy of the People*. However, in June 1881 he writes to his publisher that he has put everything else aside in order to set to work on some dramatic material which he has long been turning over in his mind, but which is now forcing itself upon him to such an extent that he can no longer let it lie. By October *Ghosts* was completed, before Christmas it had appeared as a book – and caused a scandal greater than that created by any other book in the history of Norwegian literature.

In Ibsen, the inner continuity from work to work is often marked, but never more so than between *A Doll's House*

Dengang da gaderne i min födeby Skien for en del år siden fik navne – eller kanske de bare blev omdöbte – möd jeg den are at få en gade opkaldst efter mig. Således har i alfald aviserne berettet, og jeg har hört det samme af trovardige rejsende. Efter deres forklaring skulde denne gade strakke sig fra torvet ned imod havnen eller 'Muddringen'.

40 An excerpt from Ibsen's autobiography, which he began to write in 1880, in order 'to give a factual account of the circumstances and conditions under which I wrote'. He wrote down some childhood memories, but then broke off to write *Ghosts.*

> [Some years ago, when the streets of my birthplace, Skien, were given names – or perhaps they were only rechristened – I was granted the privilege of having one of the streets called after me. That, at any rate, is what the newspapers say, though I have heard the same from reliable travellers. According to their reports, the street runs from the market place down to the harbour or 'Muddringen'.]

and the work which followed: '*Ghosts* had to be written; I could not let "the doll's house" be my last word; after Nora, Mrs Alving had to come'. In many ways Mrs Alving is an older and more mature Nora, freer yet at the same time more bound. She too wanted to break out of a marriage once, but she was sent back to her 'duties' by Pastor Manders, who thereby awakened the first doubts in her mind about transmitted doctrine. Now she has progressed far along the road which Nora wanted to explore: she has become an independent and very liberal-minded woman.

Inwardly, however, she is not free – no more so than Julian in fact: 'I am timid and afraid, because there is something of this ghostly element in me, which I can never

41   The original cover of the first edition of *Ghosts*, which was published in December 1881. *A Doll's House* was printed in a first edition of 8000 copies, but already a month later a new edition of 3000 copies had to be printed. *Ghosts*, therefore, was immediately printed in an edition of 10,000, but caused so much offence, that it was thirteen years before a new edition was necessary.

quite get rid of.' She sees the same all around her, and says that the country is full of ghosts, by which she particularly means the power that 'all sorts of old, dead ideas and all sorts of old, dead beliefs and the like' continue to exercise over the minds of the people. However, while she has been struggling to free herself intellectually, she has also been engaged in another battle and has entangled herself in lies and suppressions. By building the children's home, 'The Captain Alving Memorial Home', she has tried to rid herself of everything he left behind, to stifle all rumours of his dissolute life, and to dispose of that sum of money which once made Lieutenant Alving 'a good match'. Like Brand's mother, she has once sold herself, but unlike her she now wants to dispose of 'the purchase price'. Nothing shall be passed down to Oswald, her son, who has now become the meaning and purpose of her life: 'my son, he shall have everything from me'.

Now she has reached her goal – the children's home is to be inaugurated. The whole of the present action revolves round the inauguration, and the home becomes both a reality and a symbol. Then it emerges that the man with whom she thought she was finally finished 'has lived on as a ghost', and in Oswald who was to be exempt from all inheritance from his father. He is drawn to Regine, the full-blooded maid, just as the chamberlain was once drawn to Regine's mother. Mrs Alving has concealed from them that they are half-brother and sister. It is when she hears them out in the conservatory that for the first time in the play she uses the word 'ghosts'. Oswald has also inherited more; his father's dissolute life has left the son with an illness which at any time could reduce him to an insane human wreck. When Oswald speaks enthusiastically about that joy in work and in life which he has seen and experienced out in the world, and of his fear of staying at home – 'I am afraid that everything which wells up in me would degenerate into ugliness here' – it strikes Mrs Alving like a revelation. Her son's words bring back a memory of his father as a young man – 'in him there was joy of life, you know!' – and they pave the way for an entirely new understanding of Alving's tragedy. She sees now that it was the limiting conditions, the lack of true joy, a goal in life, and meaningful work which destroyed the best in him. She sees too that she herself was the immediate cause of his ruin, because she had made life intolerable for him with her conventional morality of duty. No sooner has she recognized this fatal causality in the family history, than she is faced with the ultimate consequences of her own guilt – Oswald's illness shows itself. As the curtain falls, she finds herself in the most desperate of all conflicts: should she – and can she – give her son the 'helping hand' which she has just promised him; can she take the life of him whom she has loved over all else, a life for which he never asked.

We never know what she chooses, and the play has been criticized for this reason: the action is not allowed to resolve itself into a conciliatory calm, according to the American literary scholar, Francis Fergusson. But whatever she does, Mrs Alving is crushed. That we never learn what she chooses, makes the effect all the stronger; the tragedy of her unresolved dilemma pursues us and is doubly gripping because, faithful to that search for knowledge and truth that is the mark of her nobility, she has so openly acknowledged her own guilt.

The development of dramatic form which we can trace from *Pillars of Society* to *A Doll's House*, continues in *Ghosts*. The handling of dialogue is more individualized and more finely attuned to the changing scenes, but it is also tauter, richer in resonances, undertones and 'dramatic irony'. The unity of time is more strictly observed. Stage set and inner action, gesture and speech, reality and symbol are yet more intimately united. Through a glass wall we see a west Norwegian fjord landscape, the changing light of which acts both as an explanation of, and as an evocative background to, what is going on between the characters. The past is made concrete in symbols, and is embodied in the figure of Oswald, while the retrospective technique is indissolubly linked to the ghost theme. Whereas in *Pillars of Society* and *A Doll's House* everything revolves round specific actions, here it is a matter of the more complex and ambiguous relationships between people. Nor, as in those two plays, does the revelation come about as the result of pressure, or intrigue between one party that wishes to reveal and one that wishes

42 Lars Nordrum and Tore Segelcke as Oswald and Mrs Alving in the second act of a Norwegian National Theatre production of *Ghosts* in 1959.

to conceal. Instead, it develops with an inner necessity, and ends in an entirely new understanding of the past, of guilt, responsibility, and causality. Furthermore, all this – the taut structure, the crushing background of nature, the marked inner connections between things great and small – contributes significantly to the impression of a remorseless retribution and a merciless fate.

The first producers regarded Oswald, the doomed young artist with his pathetic longing for beauty and joy, as the main character. But it is Mrs Alving who is struggling towards a goal, it is she who is continuously growing and battling with herself, and it is she who undergoes profound upheavals and reaches a new understanding of the situation and her own role in it. The grouping of the characters also

points to her as the central figure. She is set in relief by
Pastor Manders, a naive spokesman for the status quo. Her
personality also stands out against that of the carpenter,
Engstrand, who with his shady dealings reveals for us the
seamy side of the Manders morality, while at the same time
his conscious hypocrisy underlines the pastor's unsuspecting
naivety. However, Mrs Alving also has something in common
with Engstrand: they have both let themselves be bought in
marriage, and they have both tried to hide the truth about
their marriage partners and Regine's birth. On the other
hand, Engstrand's cunning duplicity highlights Mrs Alving's
struggle for freedom and her subjective honesty, in the same
way that his plans for the chamberlain's inheritance stand in
significant contrast to hers.

In intellectual content, and in the substance of its conflict,
Ghosts has obvious roots in the plays that preceded it, but
at the same time it goes far beyond them. The contrast
between the free world out there and the crushing conditions
at home, something that was a subsidiary element in *Pillars
of Society*, has here acquired fateful consequences. The dis-
parity between appearance and reality in a respected pillar
of the community is even more marked here than in the
earlier plays, though at the same time responsibility is more
emphatically placed on society and the established virtues.
The criticism of marriage in particular has acquired greater
depth and a broader perspective. We are brought face to
face with a society where people and feelings are bought and
sold. This leads to – and hides – a most outrageous double
standard of morality. Nor does this traffic in marriages affect
only the guilty ones, but new generations also, like original
sin.

In contrast to narrow mindedness and a double standard
of morality, *Ghosts* posits *the joy of life* as a value of the
highest order. This joy is identified with a *delight in work*,
love, and a free and creative personality, and it is set against

43 When *Ghosts* was published, it was offered to all the theatres in the Scandinavian capitals, but every one refused it. The first performance took place in Chicago in 1882, and a year later the first Scandinavian performance took place at Hälsingborg. The illustration shows August Lindberg as Oswald, and Hedvig Winter-Hjelm as Mrs Alving. The performance was shown at Møllergadens Theatre in October 1883.

the barren, joy-killing morality of duty and obedience and their consequences, hypocrisy and immorality. All the tragic fates have their origin in an innate need for the joy of life which was not given scope and never found a response. The phrase 'joy of life' was not new, but here for the first time it acquired significance in Scandinavian literature.

It is also striking that the basic philosophy in *Ghosts* is more pessimistic than in the plays immediately preceding it. *Pillars of Society* ended in an avowal of faith in truth and

44   This caricature in *Vikingen* 1881 shows the curiosity and expectation with which the public awaited the publication of *Ghosts,* and the fear which overcame them when the box with its curious contents was seen to contain a poisonous snake.

freedom, and Nora went out into the world trusting in the same forces. Mrs Alving's love of truth and freedom force her at the end to face her own responsibility, and she is confronted with a biological determinism (whatever more recent hereditary biologists may say). No one can doubt that in this area the play was influenced by Darwinism and naturalism. Even so, when Ibsen makes heredity into an agent of retribution it is neither Darwinian nor naturalistic, but genuinely Ibsenian. 'The sins of the father' are visited on Oswald, just as once they were on Brand, though now in modern 'scientific' guise.

Ghosts touched on topics, such as veneral disease, incest and mercy-killing, which had been suppressed and kept hidden from public view. It also set a large question mark against a morality based on duty, against marriage and Christianity, and ultimately against the whole of existing society. Yet all this Ibsen wanted to present on the stage. The reactions were as one might expect. The theatres said no, the literary adviser at Christiania Theatre saying that one might just as well open the hospitals to the public. One critic considered it an 'accumulation of vileness, a sewer of modern abominations', another thought that Ibsen had been mad or drunk and had written the play in a state of delirium. Andreas Munch rebuked him in a poem entitled 'A Fallen Star', and Monrad interpreted the work as an involuntary confirmation of the truths of Christianity. In an editorial article (written by Garborg), even the radical-liberal newspaper, *Dagbladet*, dissociated itself from the play. However, there were those who defended it, among them Georg Brandes and Bjørnson, Camilla Collett, Amalie Skram and Hans Jæger. In *Nyt Tidsskrift* the philosopher Arne Løchen wrote a lengthy article about 'Ibsen's basic moral philosophy', and maintained that in essence it was the same in *Ghosts* as in earlier plays. The most important contribution, however, came from P. O. Schjøtt, also in *Nyt Tidsskrift* (1882). He placed Ghosts on a par with classical drama because it was a family tragedy and social drama in one. Behind and beyond the individuals, 'society's striving and tragedy can be seen and felt, its struggle, its sufferings, its guilt and its punishment'. It is for these reasons that he called Ibsen's play 'the reincarnation of ancient tragedy in the modern world'.

The first performance took place in Chicago in 1882. A year later the play was performed by August Lindberg's private touring company in Hälsingborg and the Scandinavian capitals. The production was a triumph for the work, but as late as 1891, when it was first performed in England, the scandal surrounding Ibsen was greater than ever before. The previous year it had been staged at *Den Nationale Scene*, where Irgens Hansen was director, but it was not till 1900 that it was produced in the country's main theatre.

An Enemy of the People

Ibsen was prepared for the fact that *Ghosts* would create an uproar, and therefore, if we are to believe his own word, he took 'the critical excesses' very calmly. But he was irritated by the 'misrepresentations', and in a letter to Sophus Schandorf – who, prompted by Ibsen, published it in the Danish *Morgenbladet* – he tried to defend himself against 'all the ignorance and distortions' which the play had been exposed to. In this letter he disclaimed all responsibility for the opinions of the characters, but in other letters he did not conceal where his sympathies lay. To Olaf Skavlan he wrote, 'is it only in the field of politics that the struggle for freedom is to be permitted here at home?' and in letters to Georg Brandes he expressed his fury about those journalists who 'talk and write about freedom and liberal-mindedness, but who at the same time make themselves the slaves of the supposed opinions of their subscribers'.

If these experiences did not provide the idea for *An Enemy of the People* (1882), they did at least influence it in many ways. The action takes place in a milieu similar to that of *The League of Youth* and *Pillars of Society*. We meet the printer Aslaksen again, and hear that Stensgård has become *stift-samtmann* (diocesan governor), while the teacher Rørlund is quoted by his students. There is a strong comic atmosphere, and the structure is simple and traditional, being free from retrospective revelations, but at the same time the play is rich in memorable scenes. The symbolism is unambiguous and the character portrayal as clear as daylight.

The social criticism is more overt and aggressive than in any other Ibsen play. In Doctor Stockmann's tragi-comic struggle with the authorities, public opinion and the press on account of the threat to health posed by the baths, which are the town's chief source of income, the play sets up moral and human considerations on the one hand against bureaucratic conservatism, economic self-interest and mob appeal on the other. It exposes motivations, arguments and strategies which seem to recur in all reactions to troublesome campaigners, not just those where pollution

45 Dr Stockmann (Lasse Kolstad) speaking at the public meeting in the fourth act of *An Enemy of the People*, and shouting out to an angry audience, 'the majority is never right. Never, I tell you!' From The Norwegian Theatre production in 1973.

of the environment is concerned, though that is a subject which ninety years later has acquired a new and very real relevance.

The criticism has a further purpose. The conflict about the waters of the spa open 'endless perspectives' for the doctor: 'no, it is the whole society which needs to be cleansed, disinfected –' The complacency and opposition which he meets lead to the 'discoveries' of which he speaks at the public meeting in Act IV, saying that 'all our spiritual resources are poisoned and that the whole of our civic community rests on an infected bed of lies', that the most dangerous enemy to truth and freedom amongst us is 'the damned, compact, liberal majority'. He explains this on the basis of a radical theory of the elite: on the way to ever new truths, the loner will always be far ahead of the majority, and he locates the reason for this distance between 'those who man the outposts' and the 'spiritual masses' in the difference of cultural background and basic human quality. He expresses himself as a medical man and Darwinian biologist, and speaks of people who are like poodles and those who are like mongrels, but he does not link the words to a particular race or class. He sees a typical representative of the 'spiritual masses' in the town's highest official, his own brother, 'because he thinks what his superiors think, and believes what his superiors believe'. At the end when the doctor stakes everything on the future and intends to start a school for his own children, he asks them to go out and find some real 'street-urchins', because 'just for once, I'm going to try an experiment on the mongrels. You can find some really bright ones amongst them once in a while'. In its choice of words, this is hardly a democratic statement, but it does reveal Stockmann's hope of finding new allies outside the bourgeois class.

Doctor Stockmann, who according to Ibsen has characteristics from both Bjørnson and Jonas Lie, is one of Ibsen's most lively creations. Not only is he an undaunted champion of truth, and the hero of the work, but he is also a superb comedy figure, enthusiastic and impractical, irascible and naive, colourful in his passionate eloquence, bubbling over with fighting spirit and humour. In the right hands, this character has time and again made *An Enemy of the People* – artistically perhaps the weakest of Ibsen's plays – into entertaining theatre. Whereas the majority of early critics were cool, partly for ideological reasons, producers were soon queuing to be allowed to stage it.

That Stockmann is well on the way to being a mouthpiece for the writer, and one of the strongest expressions of his own individuality, is something Ibsen himself confirmed in a letter to his publisher, Hegel:

Dr Stockmann and I got on remarkably well together; we

agree on so many topics. But the doctor is more muddle-headed than I am, and moreover has many characteristics which enable him to say things which perhaps would not have been taken in such good part had they been said by me.

In a letter to Brandes a year later he also drew a parallel between Stockmann and his own isolated position as an 'outpost-fighter'.

Halvdan Koht reminds us that philosophers as democratic as de Tocqueville and Stuart Mill had been concerned with similar problems involving the 'tyranny of the majority' and the freedom of the individual. It should also be remembered that the majority in *An Enemy of the People* is a majority of 'all citizens entitled to vote'. Shortly after (in jottings for

46 Dr Stockmann grabs his umbrella and chases the news-paper editor Hovstad and the printer Aslaksen out of the door. Fredrik Matheson's illustration to Act V of *An Enemy of the People*, from *Three Plays of Henrik Ibsen*, New York, 1964.

The Wild Duck) Ibsen notes, 'what silly fools! They assert the right of the majority, and yet those qualified to vote are only a small and arbitrarily limited minority'. This is perhaps the draft of a reply, but in letters to Bjørnson in the midst of the shift of power in 1884 he certainly speaks on his own account. He does not expect any great results from the change, for those who have 'political, local and social privileges' will not of their own free will share them with 'the unprivileged majority'. He hopes, therefore, that 'all the unprivileged' will form their own strong and determined party with an extensive programme of practical reforms, including among other things radically extended suffrage and 'the emancipation of popular education from all kinds of medievalism'. Fourteen years later, when a journalist reminded him of Stockmann's words, Ibsen remarked, 'I am not responsible for all the nonsense he proclaims'.

Like Stockmann, Ibsen was on his way, and in his next play he had already left *An Enemy of the People* far behind him in more than one sense.

The Wild Duck

In September 1884 Ibsen sent the manuscript of *The Wild Duck* to his publisher, and in the accompanying letter said that 'in some ways this new work occupies a place apart in my dramatic production, the method of procedure differing in several respects from my earlier one'. He also prophesied that 'the study and rendering of these people' on the stage would not be easy, and that the critics would find 'plenty to squabble about, plenty to interpret'. His prophesy came true. Contemporary critics were confused, the public likewise, and later actors, critics and scholars have interpreted the work in widely differing ways.

It was not, however, Ibsen's intention to mystify. He knew what he wanted, and he hoped to be understood. He had detailed discussions with Schrøder, the director of the

47 'Henrik Ibsen as castigator'. Caricature in *Vikingen* 1882. Ibsen impales Stensgård from *The League of Youth*, while the conservatives rub their hands with delight. Below, Bernick from *Pillars of Society* gets a kick in the pants to the obvious delight of the liberals. But then in the figure of Dr Stockmann, he wields his whip to both Right and Left.

Christiania Theatre, about the casting of the play, stressed that both ensemble and staging demanded 'naturalness and realism in every aspect', and placed particular emphasis on the lighting: 'it is different in every act, and designed to correspond to the basic mood which gives each of the five acts its own special character'.

This last feature is far better sustained and far more subtly worked out than in any of the earlier Ibsen dramas, even though lighting was also important in *Ghosts*. However, one can hardly say that the use of lighting is different in *The Wild Duck*. Where there is a difference is in the social setting, the use of symbols and attitude. Whereas all Ibsen's other modern plays are set in well-to-do bourgeois or academic circles, four of the five acts of this play are set in a lower middle-class milieu, in a family in difficult and economically dependent circumstances. The family is portrayed with an intimacy which is unique in Ibsen, and with a concern for the characteristic features both of the interior and in the use of language. Never has he been more realistic than here, and yet in the midst of the realism there is the central symbol. This subtle blending of scenic realism and poetic symbolism is one of the most important innovations in the play.

In *Ghosts* too the title points to the main symbol, but there despite everything it is only a metaphor. The wild duck, on the other hand, is a real bird, which for good reasons is not visible, but is nonetheless a part of the reality depicted on the stage, for we know that it lives in the strange forest of Christmas trees there in the loft. It is of significance to the plot, while at the same time both it and the loft acquire an ever richer symbolic content, with obvious, half-hidden or possible links with nearly all the characters in the work. In addition it is charged with meaning and is a vital element in the creation of mood.

All the same, the most daring feature of the play is the sustained combination of tragedy and comedy. There are comic elements in the tragedy of *Ghosts*, and we glimpse tragic possibilities in the comedy of *An Enemy of the People*, but only in *The Wild Duck* do the tragic and comic elements fuse. Comedy or farce scenes, such as the breakfast scene in Act III, can take place between profoundly serious ones, but the same scene can also contain comic and pathetic elements, and at the end even the death scene is tinged with a macabre humour. *The Wild Duck* is a tragi-comedy, as Ibsen himself described it, and it is so in the deepest sense of the word: human life and the human condition consistently seen in a double perspective.

The core of the tragedy, as of the comedy, lies in the clash between Gregers Werle's idealism, his talk of the 'claims of the ideal', and the reality to which he directs them. It was here that 'the method of procedure' was most 'different' and therefore most confusing for Ibsen's contemporaries. That the idealist and proclaimer of the truth should come into conflict with his surroundings, was normal for an Ibsen play, but here it was as if everything was turned upside-down.

If one looks at the structure of the play, it becomes evident that Gregers Werle is both the main character and the one who carries the action. He sets himself a noble task, that of rescuing Hjalmar Ekdal from lies and concealment. He pursues his task, overcomes all obstacles, and reveals to Hjalmar 'the truth' about his marriage to Gina. But he is defeated in that 'the truth' does not have the intended effect, but on the contrary poisons Hjalmar's relations not only with Gina, but even more with Hedvig – and with catastrophic results. Perhaps Gregers will draw the ultimate conclusion from his mistakes and his 'destiny': 'to be the thirteenth at table'.

In this way we can trace a basically tragic element through the play, one that is linked to Gregers Werle. From one point of view, it is even possible to see him as a tragic hero, the idealist who suffers defeat against a wretched reality, and the

48   Gregers Werle and Hedvig in Act III. Hedvig is retouching photographs for her father, the photographer, Hjalmar Ekdal. From a Dresden production of *The Wild Duck* during the inter-war years.

play has been interpreted and played in this way. But from the beginning the motives behind his idealism reveal themselves to be somewhat mixed in character, and one of the strongest is the need to assuage a sick conscience, not by his own sacrifices, but by intervening in the lives of others with his excessive demands. Nor is it beyond question that in all things he represents the truth, or that he interprets the past correctly. He is so blinded by his own needs, and by what Dr Relling calls his 'fits of hero-worship', that he gravely misjudges those he wishes to help. He overestimates Hjalmar Ekdal in a way which casts a comic light on what one could otherwise call his tragic blindness, and he leads Hedvig into ways of thinking that bring about her shocking and tragic, though – if Relling is right – pointless, sacrificial death. It is she, not Gregers, who pays the price of his idealism and his fateful miscalculations.

That is how mercilessly the sick roots of the idealist's preaching are exposed, and are highlighted by their effects. Gregers' idealism is also accurately diagnosed by Dr Relling, who may be a cynic without illusions, but who nevertheless shows, particularly in what he says about Hedvig, that he understands people. The milieu into which Gregers intrudes, on the other hand, is characterized by simple human values, warmth and mutual concern, and the characters are presented with humour and tolerant understanding despite their failings. Hjalmar Ekdal, who is the most colourful and vital character in the play, is certainly wretched and laughable, weak, ridiculous, spoilt and irresponsible, full of excuses and

49 Alarmed, Gina Ekdal (Mona Hofland) backs away when the merchant, Werle (Claes Gill), unexpectedly calls at their studio flat in Act III of *The Wild Duck*. The New Theatre, Oslo, 1968.

self-dramatizing phrases, lazy and cowardly, and given to dreams which in his heart of hearts he does not believe. But he is also a charming dilettante artist, a good father and in his own egocentric way a good husband, who is happy in his simple but cosy home. Ibsen has definitely exposed him, but he felt very strongly that the comic sides should not be overplayed. As he wrote to Schrøder:

> This part must not be played with any parody in the rendering, nor with any indication that the actor is aware of anything comical in his remarks. He has, as Relling says, a very winning voice, and this above all else must be maintained. His sentimentality is genuine, his melancholy charming in its way – not the least bit affected. I would like, in confidence, to draw your attention to Kristofer Janson, who can be quite simply delightful even when he is talking utter nonsense.

Old Ekdal too has his obvious faults, but a certain dignity nonetheless. Gina is down-to-earth and practical, also somewhat comical, and totally without feeling for the heroic gesture, but despite this, quietly heroic in her everyday struggle. Dr Rank too has his redeeming features and his weak spot. Above all, however, Hedvig – she is named after Ibsen's sister – is drawn with a tenderness that is rare in Ibsen's writing, with a deep understanding of the distinctive quality of her soul and her peculiar situation, her love, her dreams and her self-sacrifice. She is not idealized, but is a living poetic creation which shines all the brighter in its trivial surroundings. She possesses a tragic greatness which transcends the gloomy realities of the world in which she lives.

In the centre of this circle stands the wild duck. It is of decisive significance for the action, but at the same time it is a symbol. The basis for the symbolic value which Gregers Werle ascribes to it lies in the fact that it is not living in its natural environment, that it is wounded, and that in

popular belief wounded wild ducks dive to the bottom and
there hold on with their beaks. It thus becomes an image of
the need wounded people have to cling to illusions. In this
way Gregers associates it both with old Ekdal and with
Hjalmar. It is tempting for a reader or audience to draw
further parallels, with Molvik and Relling – and Gregers
himself. The relationship to Hedvig is different, and this was
probably the original one for the writer, for in the draft it
says, '– Hedvig as wild duck –' For her the duck is primarily
a living creature, strange and foreign, but she also feels a
mysterious affinity with it, senses that they share a common
fate, and dies the death that was intended for it. It is the
same with the loft in which the duck lives. For old Ekdal it
is a substitute for the open-air life he once led, for Hjalmar
a refuge when everyday life becomes too difficult, and for
Gregers an image of false reality, a caricature of the free life
he knows from the Høydal forests. For Hedvig, however, it is
something quite different. She does not seek refuge there from
a greater and richer reality, instead she seeks and finds such
a reality in the loft, in everything frightening and fascinating,
death and life, 'churches and palaces and streets and big ships
sailing on the sea'. All the strange things in there, in 'the
depths of the sea', as she calls it, speaks to her childlike
imagination, while at the same time she – in contrast to her
father and grandfather – has the child's sharp and natural
sense of reality, 'for of course it's only a loft'.

In this way the duck and the loft serve directly and
indirectly to characterize the individuals and their various
attitudes to life. They reflect a reality which is complex and
rich in contrasts, and which the play opposes to a narrow,
categorical moralism. They broaden the perspective, become
a poetic, focal and ambiguous image of life as the majority
of us live it in this imperfect world.

Many have seen *The Wild Duck* as an expression of a change
in Ibsen's writing, as a reaction against the works im-

50   The final scene of *The Wild Duck* at the Christiania Theatre in January 1885. Gina (Lucie Wolf) and Hjalmar Ekdal (Arnoldus Reimers) carry the dead Hedvig (Lully Krohn) into her room. Old Ekdal (Johannes Brun), Gregers Werle (Hjalmar Hammer) and Dr Relling (Andreas Isachsen) stand in the background. Bjørn Bjørnson had directed the production, and Ibsen had commented that 'it is difficult to imagine that anyone could have done it better'.

mediately preceding it, a confrontation with the zeal for truth, and a resigned recognition of the necessity of illusions and the 'life lie'. But *The Wild Duck* does not invalidate Stockmann's criticism of the lies and deceit of those in power. Here it is a matter of something else: the modest happiness of individuals wounded by life, set against alien ideals; and of their right to live their own lives, 'undisturbed by these confounded hawkers who keep banging on the doors of us poor folk with the claims of the ideal'. As Ibsen wrote to Theodor Caspari while he was still working on the play, 'I have long ago stopped making universally valid demands, because I no longer believe that one has any inherent right to make them. I am of the opinion that the best and only thing anyone of us can do, is to try to realize ourselves in spirit and in truth'.

To the extent that *The Wild Duck* reflects a growing

scepticism, and recognition of the mutability and relativity of truth, it continues a trend already established in Ibsen's earlier plays. The work may take a snipe at the abstract zeal for truth, but at the same time it extends the demand for truth in that it defends the claims of reality against ideals that are remote from life. Looked at in this way, *The Wild Duck* becomes part of the struggle which realism and naturalism waged against the idealism which was a heritage from romanticism, and which in Ibsen reached a peak in *Brand*. At the same time, the profound psychological insights and the imaginative and poetic use of symbols point towards the 'neo-romanticism' and 'symbolism' of the 1890s.

Does *The Wild Duck* indicate that Ibsen has abandoned all idealism and lost all faith in people? Has he once and for all characterized all high aims, all ideal demands, as a camouflage for purely personal motivation? Is Gregers Werle the beginning of an ongoing exposure of the tragic 'hero'?

There are critics and scholars who believe this. Others maintain that even after *The Wild Duck*, Ibsen's main characters are inspired by high ideals, but that they often suffer defeat because – as so many before them – they have incurred guilt or betrayed themselves. Despite this, their downfall becomes a triumph for the ideals which they nevertheless believe in and which they affirm by their death.

A case can be made for both these points of view, but there is also a third, namely that the circumstances are more complicated, and that it changes from work to work and character to character, and is an expression of the continuous struggle and uninterrupted dialogue between opposing forces in the writer himself, those of doubt and faith, idealism and sceptical realism. The account which follows is based on this view.

'Human beings, human emotions and human destinies'

Rosmersholm

During the summer of 1885, Ibsen was in Norway for the first time in eleven years, and this new meeting with his home country was to leave deep traces in the works which followed. He heard the *Storting* debate about an author's stipend for Kielland. This confirmed his suspicion that the 'liberals' were not as broad-minded as they had claimed to be, and in a speech to the workers of Trondhjem, he spoke of his disappointment that freedom of speech and freedom of conscience did not have better safeguards under the 'new form of government' – parliamentary democracy, which had been introduced with the change of regime the year before. Nor did he believe that 'our present democracy' could manage the task, but maintained that 'an element of nobility' would have to be brought into the administration, the country's representative bodies and the press:

> I am obviously not thinking of a nobility of birth, nor one of wealth, nor one of knowledge – not even one of talent and abilities. I am thinking of one of character, a nobility of mind and will. This alone can liberate us.

He prophesied that this nobility would come from the women and workers, and he pointed to the transformation of society, and the position of these two groups in particular, which was now being planned out in Europe, 'that is what I am hoping for and waiting for, and what I will work for, as far as I am able'.

The two months he spent in Molde were a somewhat more cheerful interlude, but by the time he left Norway he had been able to experience the bitter party struggles at close quarters. He came into conflict with the conservative committee of *Studentersamfundet* (The Student Society), where his old friend Lorentz Dietrichson was president, and he was violently attacked by the right-wing press.

That impressions and experiences from the trip to Norway formed the basis of *Rosmersholm*, is something Ibsen admitted to both Hegel and Brandes when the play was completed in the autumn of 1886, and even if some preliminary drafts predate that, there is no reason to doubt his word. For one thing, the Norwegian politics of the day, and Ibsen's own political attitude, have left stronger marks on *Rosmersholm* than on any other of his plays. With a few words about 'the government of the moment' in headmaster Kroll's right-wing paper, the play is immediately placed in the period after 1884. The headmaster himself is a typical example of the conservative official class after the change of power, stiff-necked and intransigent, while the editor, Peder Mortensgård, is a wily spokesman for the right wing of the Left – spiritually akin to the printer Aslaksen in *An Enemy of the People*. Rosmer, on the other hand, has broken with his conservative friends, and speaks, much as Ibsen did, of working for 'the true democracy', which would have as its task that of 'making all my countrymen noblemen'. When, horrified by the brutality of the political struggle, he wishes to bring redress, he reacts as the writer himself did – though with the important difference that he wants to reconcile the opposing forces, while Ibsen put his hope in new groups and classes.

The political differences are indissolubly linked to the differences in attitude to life and basic philosophy – something which again corresponds to the actual situation, though here simplified and accentuated. More clearly than in any other modern drama we see the pattern from *Emperor and Galilean*. On the one hand there is the Christian tradition, represented by the Rosmer family, the dead Beate Rosmer and the headmaster, Kroll – and to a certain extent also by Mortensgård. On the other, there is the radical, pagan liberalism of Rebecca West, and behind her the dead Dr West, and on the periphery of everything, Rosmer's first teacher, Ulrik Brendel, the 'sybarite', 'epicure', and vaga-bond philosopher. The opposing forces wrestle for control in Rosmer, who has resigned his clerical vocation – he is an 'apostate' like Julian – but more and more so in Rebecca also, while the idea of 'the third kingdom' can be glimpsed in Rosmer's free and happy noblemen, and acquires visionary strength and intensity in his dream of reconciliation and a new society:

> Oh, what a joy it would be to live then. No more hateful strife. Only friendly rivalry. All eyes fixed on the same goal, every will, every mind straining forwards – up-wards –, each one in the way determined by his own nature. Happiness for all – created by all.

An Enemy of the People ended at the point where Stockman wanted to go out and liberate the minds of men, and that – as Georg Brandes says – is where *Rosmersholm* begins. To that extent *Rosmersholm* stands in the same relation to *An Enemy of the People* as *Ghosts* does to *A Doll's House*; while with regard to theme, milieu-description and dramatic structure, *Rosmers-holm* and *Ghosts* are themselves closely related. Here, how-ever, the conflicting forces are far more bitterly opposed, and far more deeply rooted in the mind.

The west Norwegian estate of Rosmersholm reminds one of Mrs Alving's Rosenvold, but is far more strongly identified with the power of the past. For hundreds of years the same family of officials, clergymen, officers and others has con-tinued to live here. This is historically inconceivable, but the writer has gone beyond the bounds of realism in order to focus as much traditional, physical and spiritual power in one place as possible. The estate has become a symbol. Kroll calls it a stronghold of 'everything that is believed and acknowledged by the best people in our society': according to Rosmer, it has been the place from which the Rosmer family has spread 'darkness and oppression down through the years'. The deceased ancestors are, as it were, present on stage: they stare down on the living from paintings, and quell both laughter and tears at birth. Mrs Helseth speaks of 'the white horse', an image which bears the stamp of myth and age-old belief, a suggestive symbol of death and the power of the dead. From the start, Rebecca is visually associated with this symbol on account of the white shawl which she is crocheting. Above all, however, it is Beate Rosmer, who sought her death in the mill-race, who now exercises power over those living at Rosmersholm. The footbridge which she jumped from both terrifies and lures, and from beginning to end the dialogue revolves in ever tighter circles round the events preceding her suicide. When they have all been brought to light, the seal is also set on the tragedy of the main characters: 'Mrs Rosmer took them'.

Beate's counterpart is Rebecca, Rebecca as she was when she came to Rosmersholm, driven by a dauntless will, with courage to grasp life and happiness, and heedless of any standards or codes of behaviour other than her own. She has largely succeeded in freeing Rosmer from the power of tradition, and in opening for him 'the great world of truth and freedom'. He has her full support for the life-task he now wants to take up, and his great vision combines her dream of freedom and happiness with his own ethical idealism. At the end of Act II when he asks her if she is willing to become his wife, she exults with a joy which reveals that this has been her secret ambition, but the next moment she turns round violently and rejects all thought of taking Beate's place. The remainder of the play explains why: she for her part has begun to be influenced by Rosmer and 'the Rosmer philosophy of life', and she has begun to experience guilt. Her reactions rebound on to Rosmer: he begins to doubt whether he was as free from guilt concerning Beate's death as he has hitherto believed, and immediately after his words about the new society, a change takes place in him, similar to the earlier one in Rebecca: 'any cause that is to win a lasting victory, must be led by a happy and guiltless man'.

Rebecca still tries to keep up Rosmer's courage and will, but when Kroll succeeds in arousing her suspicion that the Dr West to whom she owes all her ideas and with whom she has, apparently, had a relationship, was her father, then something snaps in her. To exonerate Rosmer from all guilt, she confesses how by hints and suggestions she lured Beate on to the path which led to the mill-race, and how later she herself was driven by 'a wild uncontrollable passion', as irresistible as a storm at sea in her native northern Norway. Rosmer is shocked, and even though Rebecca goes on to explain how their spiritual life together has transformed and 'ennobled' her, but broken her will and killed her capacity for happiness, he can no longer believe in her or in his own ability to ennoble others. He demands proof, and half against his will, impelled by just such 'a horrible fascination' as was Rebecca in relation to Beate, he urges her to take the path Beate took. Symbolically he takes her hand in marriage, and together as man and wife they go to their death 'gladly'. Rebecca has been totally won over by 'the Rosmer philosophy of life' and by the idea of atonement, while Rosmer, who has wavered in his faith in 'our emancipated view of life', reaffirms it: 'there is no judge over us. Therefore we will have to judge ourselves'.

Rosmersholm begins politically and develops into a drama of ideas about conflicting attitudes and philosophies of life. 'But first and foremost the play is of course about human beings and human destinies', as Ibsen said in a letter to a discussion group of grammar school students. A profound

51 Rebecca West (Astrid Folstad), the headmaster Kroll (Arne Bang-Hansen) and Rosmer (Knut Wigert) in Act III of *Rosmersholm*. Rebecca wants to free Rosmer from guilt, so tells him that it was she who lured Beate – Rosmer's wife and Kroll's sister – 'on to the paths which led to the mill-race'. Norwegian National Theatre production 1963.

human tragedy, it is a drama about a political-idealistic undertaking which comes to nothing because the gaze is turned inwards and backwards, with spiritual revolutions and crippling self knowledge as the only result. The course of the play itself illustrates Ibsen's development away from a socially critical to a purely psychological dramaturgy.

The tragedy of Rebecca and Rosmer portrays characters

more complex, and plumbs deeper into the subconscious, repressed life of the spirit than anything Ibsen had previously written. The exposure of past events interacts with what takes place in the present to reveal not only hidden actions, but also hidden motives, and transforms the characters before our eyes. The development which Rebecca has undergone and the conflicts which are still present in her: the desire for life and the willingness to sacrifice, her winning personality and its dangerous depths, the open and the mysterious, the transformation which both ennobles and kills – all these qualities make her one of the most exciting women characters in world drama. Despite her uniqueness she still represents something universal: the tragic paradox of the individual in whom emancipation from accepted standards has gone so far that she has nothing with which to resist when the forces of nature rise up in her, and she loses control of her own life. Rosmer, in many ways her counterpart, is also complex and tragic, a visionary dreamer, upright and refined, who, as Ibsen wrote to Schrøder, must be played by 'the best and most sensitive actor the theatre has at its disposal'. However, he is also weak and hesitant, tormented by 'familial doubt, familial fear, familial scruples', and ultimately defenceless against them. That is why he feels all the more strongly the need for happiness and freedom, but also the fear of action and passion. Deep down there are dangerous poten-tialities in him too, for 'the demonic' as it is called in the notes for the play, and which break out in the last act.

To a large extent *Rosmersholm* is a drama about the influence of surroundings on the human mind, and about the influence of one mind on another. Rebecca contains the moods of the sea and the nature of Finnmark in her own being, just as Rosmer is permeated by the spirit of Rosmers-holm. The people too shape and transform each other, not just by word and deed, but by purely psychical influence, ranging from involuntary 'infection' to conscious suggestion.

This is the way Rebecca has influenced Beate and Rosmer, and the way Rosmer influences Rebecca. Likewise, it is just as much through his being as through his strange speech that at decisive moments Ulrik Brendel becomes involved in the action. Similarly the symbols are more than images for spiritual realities, for they acquire a suggestive power over people – the mill-race, the white horses.

However, it was precisely because the play is so complex, that it was so little understood when it first appeared. It is true that Edvard Brandes called it a masterpiece, but the majority of critics were cool, and sales were slow. By contrast, later generations, from Sigmund Freud who wrote a penetrating essay about Rebecca West, to the general theatre public, have been deeply fascinated by the play.

The Lady from the Sea

Those elements of nature mysticism, folklore, myth and irrational forces which in *Rosmersholm* break through for the first time since *Peer Gynt*, reappear, and are far more prominent in *The Lady from the Sea*, which was written two years later. The title and several bits of dialogue link the main character, Ellida Wangel, with mermaids of folklore. As Pavel Fraenkl has shown, the plot is a variation on the old theme, which Ibsen must have known from legends and ballads, of the lost or dead bridegroom who seeks out his faithless bride and demands her return. We also catch a glimpse of another motif, that of the woman who is rescued from the clutches of the water-sprite or sea-troll.

However, the play is securely rooted in reality. As Ibsen himself had said the year before to William Archer, his English translator and enthusiastic champion, life itself is full of symbols. When Ellida Wangel claims that the stranger has occult powers, and characteristics which indicate a super-natural origin, this belief is to a large extent conditioned by her own state of mind. Even though he – like Ulrik

Brendel – appears at a moment of great psychological tension, and remains shrouded in mystery, there is nothing supernatural about his behaviour on stage. The setting resembles a corner of Molde in summer, something Ibsen had experienced a couple of years before. It is colourfully drawn, but free from those satirical elements which otherwise characterize Ibsen's pictures of provincial life. The greater part of the action takes place out of doors – in contrast to the entire succession of plays from *Pillars of Society* to *Rosmersholm* – and the carp pond in the foreground, and the fjord in the distance, are both drawn into the web of symbols and images, in which the sea is the dominating element.

Ellida Wangel is even more bound to the sea and to the past than Rebecca West was, but for her they are one and the same power. She constantly feels 'this compelling homesickness for the sea'. According to Wangel she 'belongs among sea people', and she herself believes that the human race should really have lived in or on the sea; for 'then we would be perfect in a way quite different from what we are now. Both better and happier'. She is of the opinion that the deepest reason for our human unhappiness lies in the fact that we became land instead of sea animals.

The sea is intimately associated with her own past, with her childhood, and particularly with the foreign seaman to whom she once pledged her word, and to whom she bound herself symbolically when they joined rings and threw them into the sea. She is constantly seeking the sea, bathes at all times of the day, and lives as a stranger with her husband and his two daughters. In notes for the play it states quite clearly: 'the secret in her marriage, that which she hardly dares admit to herself, hardly dares think about: the compelling power exercised on her imagination by the other one. The lost one. Ultimately – in the involuntary imagination – it is with him that she lives her married life'. The longing for the sea expresses her repressed erotic attraction to the

52   The Stranger (Johan Norlund) has come to ask Ellida (Tore Segelcke) if she will accompany him, but she draws back, afraid, and seeks protection with her husband, Dr Wangel (Børseth Rasmussen). Act III, Scene III, of the Norwegian National Theatre production of *The Lady from the Sea* in 1952.

stranger. In the midst of the crisis she herself sees the connection, 'oh, Wangel, – save me from myself! (...) That which draws me is just behind. (...) That man is like the sea'.

In contrast to Rebecca, Ellida is saved. When 'he who was lost' returns, the crisis becomes acute. She is drawn towards him, but at the same time retreats, terrified, 'the horrible, it is that which both terrifies and fascinates'. Dr Wangel tries to hold her with all the means in his power, and it is not until he sets her absolutely free that she becomes inwardly free and *therefore* responsible, a new and independent person who can face the conflict squarely and is free to choose, 'there is – transformation in this'.

In 1930 the psychiatrist Ragnar Vogt wrote that the play is

'(...) an excellent demonstration of a psycho-analytical cure', and the way in which Ibsen has here anticipated Freud, and perhaps even inspired him, has been further discussed by others. However, *The Lady from the Sea* is not to be reduced to a unique case history, for the 'cure' is brought to life with concentrated and subtle dramatic skill, and both the sea symbolism and the substrata of folklore and myth extend and universalize the perspective. As Jonas Lie wrote to Ibsen, Ellida stands at 'the only gate which can redeem us to a higher state, namely free choice'; the drama leads us to 'a border station where the choice is between spirit and nature'.

However, the play also tells of values that are lost in the freeing of oneself from the power of the terrifying to gain ethical freedom and responsibility. The sea is not only dangerous and terrifying, it is also 'the unknown', 'the boundless' and 'unattainable', and Ellida's experience of it is suffused with poetry. Nor is the ending simply happy: summer is drawing to its close, the last tourist boat is leaving, and 'soon all the sea lanes will be closed'. And there is something ambiguous in the closing refrain of Ballested, the handyman. He says it killed the mermaid to come on to dry land, but 'human beings, on the other hand – they can accom-acc-ommodate themselves'.

The retrospective main plot is supplemented by ongoing secondary intrigues. The school principal, Arnholm, proposes to Bolette in more or less the same way that Wangel once did to Ellida, and Bolette's capitulation in a way explains Ellida's. The wooing of Bolette and Hilde by the sculptor, Lyngstrand, is more loosely integrated into the overall pattern, but it casts an ironic light on artistic egotism, and contains the seed of Ibsen's 'late works'.

On the whole, *The Lady from the Sea* was well received both at home and abroad. In a series of newspaper articles Alfr. Sinding-Larsen wrote a detailed analysis of the characters and emphasized that they all had certain 'winning' qualities. Ibsen was pleased with these articles and they were later published as a book. However, many found the play obscure, and the then young Knut Hamsun made fun of 'the so splendidly enigmatic scribbling which began with *The Wild Duck* and recently culminated in that elevated madness called *The Lady from the Sea*'. The play is among those which have been better understood with the passing of time. Lately it has even been criticized for being far too obvious!

Hedda Gabler

The symbolism and mysticism of *Rosmersholm* and *The Lady from the Sea* extend the realism and to a certain degree point beyond it. *Hedda Gabler*, which appeared in 1890, the very year of the breakthrough of 'neo-romanticism' in Norwegian literature, is realistic in a far stricter sense, and resembles *A Doll's House* far more than any of the intervening plays. What symbolism there is, is largely limited to purely visual effects or 'visual suggestion' (see p. 119). Ibsen has placed more emphasis on them in this play than in any other, and, as John Northam has shown, they are used with great skill and theatrical understanding. The dividing of the stage into an outer and an inner room, General Gabler's portrait and pistols, Tesman's slippers, the colour and abundance of Hedda Gabler's and Thea Elvsted's hair – all are forms of symbolism which suggest and underline, but at the same time they are all elements which are rooted in concrete, scenic reality.

In a letter to his French translator, Moritz Prozor, Ibsen said that he did not really want to discuss 'so-called problems', but 'to describe human beings, human emotions and human destinies on the basis of certain prevailing social conditions and views'. To a German newspaper he put it another way, 'I have tried to describe people, to describe them as exactly as possible, and in as much detail as possible, nothing more. It is possible that some people will see something revolutionary in the play, but that remains in the background'.

Hedda Gabler is based on the perceptive observation of living models – among them the young Emilie Bardach (see p. 165) – and on the profound psychological study of those characters which as a result of this direct observation appeared before the writer's inner eye. He has left more jottings on Hedda than on any other character in his whole authorship. One of them says, 'it is the lack of any purpose in her life which torments her'.

When she was young, Hedda had tried to participate in Ejlert Løvborg's life by persuading him to tell her about his bohemian excesses. She had, however, drawn back when he desired her as a woman, and she admits now, many years later, that it was from cowardice. Instead, she had let herself slip into a marriage with Tesman, the erudite but immature and unimaginative 'specialist', and she now finds herself caught in a petit bourgeois triangle which is a far remove from her aristocratic habits and demands.

It is in this situation that she meets Løvborg again, after the self-sacrificing Thea Elvsted has set him on the straight and narrow once more, and has 'inspired' him to write his daring work about 'the course of culture' and 'the cultural forces' of the future. Because of this, Thea not only arouses Hedda's jealousy, but brings her face to face with her own impotence and inner poverty, and precisely for this reason releases the urge in her, for once in her life, to 'have control over a human destiny'. Hedda lures Løvborg out of the anxious care with which Thea surrounds him, and goads him to seek out the temptations which at all costs Thea wants to keep him away from. 'I see him before me. With vine-leaves in his hair. Flushed and free. (...) For then you see – then he will have gained control over himself again. Then he will be a free man for the remainder of his time.'

53 A scene from the second act of *Hedda Gabler*. Hedda
Gabler (Mona Hofland) has placed herself strategically between Thea Elvsted (Eva Henning) and Ejlert Løvborg (Arne
Aas), and tries with her poisonous remarks to destroy their
relationship. After Løvborg has declined a glass of wine, Hedda
turns to Thea and says, 'there, isn't that what I told you when
you came here this morning in such a state of anxiety –' The
New Theatre, Oslo, 1966.

It is when he disappoints her faith that she gives him the
pistols and urges him to die beautifully. She, meanwhile,
burns the manuscript, Thea's and his 'child'. But Løvborg
disappoints her dream of beauty too, for the shot does not
hit him in the head, but in the abdomen. She has lost yet
again, 'oh, the laughable and the paltry, they settle like a
curse on everything I even touch'. Furthermore, she is now in
the power of the cynical judge, Brack. The final scene has
both irony and pathos; Tesman and Mrs Elvsted quickly
settle down to reconstructing Løvborg's manuscript, and
Hedda asks, 'is there nothing you two can use me for?' The
reply, 'no, nothing at all', pronounces the sentence: useless

54   In 1925 the Swedish actress, Pauline Brunius, visited the
Central Theatre, Oslo, in the role of Hedda. Here, she gives
Ejlert Løvborg (Erling Drangsholt) her pistol, and lets him
understand that he ought to take his life – but that he should
do it beautifully. Final scene of Act III.

and superfluous. She, however, shoots herself in the temple.
For the first time she defies scandal and shocks even judge
Brack, 'but, good lord, people don't do such things!'

Hedda Gabler is paralysed to the very roots of her being
by the upper-class, aristocratic-authoritarian male society of
which her father, General Gabler, is a typical representative.
The conventions of the aristocracy have become part of her
own nature, and the need for freedom and the ability to
love have been crushed by her fear of scandal. As it says in
the notes, 'there is profound poetry in Hedda, but her
surroundings frighten her. Just imagine making oneself

laughable'. But the problem goes deeper than that. As Ibsen indicates, 'it is really the whole life of a man that she wants to lead'. The General's daughter was brought up as if she were his son – she rides and shoots. She wishes to participate in Løvborg's male excesses, but at a safe distance. She cannot accept that she is pregnant, and she burns the manuscript with the words, 'now I am burning – burning your child'. As the psychologist Ingjald Nissen says, she in this way protests against the very role of woman. Nor is she able to work, or sacrifice herself for others, and thereby give her life a meaning, as Thea Elvsted and old Aunt Julie have done. She gropes after a purpose in life, dreams of beauty, and seizes the opportunity of power – but all in vain, and more and more despairingly, recklessly and destructively. In this way she is unable to find an outlet for her thirst for life, her abilities, her poetry.

As Ibsen notes, '(. . .) it is that which is suppressed in H., her hysteria, which really is the motivating force behind all her actions'. Is she, therefore just a psychiatric case – the sick product of a sick society – and masterly proof of the depth of Ibsen's psychological insight?

She has at any rate many characteristics which point beyond the individual, and are typical of the period. She is in many ways Nora's opposite. But she has many relatives in Ibsen's plays, from Hjørdis to Rebecca West; and in contemporary literature: Flaubert's Madame Bovary, Tolstoy's Anna Karenina, the 'superfluous' women in Turgenyev, Amalie Skram's Constance Ring, Strindberg's Miss Julie and Helene ('On Payment', *Marriage II*) – all of them well-to-do women, who in the society of the day were condemned to passivity. Despite this, the majority of contemporary critics found her incomprehensible and unreal, presumably because her real motives – and therefore the inner coherence of her character – are so often masked. Great actors, however, have brought her to life and modern psychology has opened the way to our understanding and recognition. The American scholar, Orley I. Holtan, maintains that eighty years after the publication of the play, such women are still to be found in American and European suburbs.

After Brand, no other Ibsen character has been more discussed than Hedda Gabler. Henrik Jæger, the first to write about her in any depth, saw in her 'a magnificent, richly endowed woman', 'a tragic character', 'a Hjørdis in corsets'. Georg Brandes, on the other hand, called her 'a truly degenerate type, without competence or real ability', while Ibsen's German biographer, Emil Reich, saw her as a satirical portrait of a modern society lady. It is between these extremes that evaluations of her have tended to move. Else Høst, however, who has written a whole book on the play, takes Jæger's evaluation as her starting point and goes so far as to say that Hedda belongs among Ibsen's tragic heroes, that she is the bearer of a dream of beauty and perfection which is expressed in the symbol 'vine-leaves in the hair', and that she seeks death because the dream cannot be realized. Others – among them Sigmund Skard and Paulus Svendsen – have replied by saying that Hedda does not have the human dimensions necessary for a tragic hero, and that the 'vine-leaves' fantasies do not stand for anything important to her, but, like her desire for power, are the expression of a warped longing for life. Yet the majority would probably agree that possibilities, longings and perhaps – in Ibsen's own words – even 'a profound poetry' are lost with the death of Hedda.

That in Ejlert Løvborg Ibsen wanted to portray a major talent, is something that few would dispute; he is a daring thinker with burning longings and a vision that penetrates far into the future. However, it is one of the weaknesses of the otherwise so well integrated play that Løvborg never gives us a glimpse of his greatness, and that we must be content with Tesman's testimony. In his notes, Ibsen does tell us a little about what the brilliant dissertation was to contain; among other things Løvborg has imagined a relationship between man and woman based on 'comradeship, from which the truly spiritual person could emerge' – an idea which points towards 'the third kingdom'. We dimly perceive the dream of such comradeship behind his relations with Hedda and Thea Elvsted, but neither Hedda's curiosity and defensive 'companionship in a common lust for life', nor Thea's platonic and correct friendship, which has broken his 'defiance and courage to live', corresponds to his deepest longings. He ends up at the house of a third woman, 'Mademoiselle Diana'. Ultimately he is a stranger in the reality which surrounds him. Again to borrow from Ibsen's jottings, 'life on the basis of the present social set-up is not worth living'. It is for this reason that Løvborg is drawn towards the 'bohemians' and eventually goes to rack and ruin. Both he and Hedda die as victims of 'social conditions and attitudes' which are too narrow to encompass their talents and peculiarities. It is here that one may locate the 'something revolutionary (...) in the background'.

'– judgement day over oneself'

Since his visit to Norway in 1885, Ibsen had again been living in Munich. In 1891, however, he moved home to Norway, went on a trip all the way up to the North Cape, and then settled in Christiania (Oslo), which from then on he made his home.

During his last years abroad, Ibsen could take pleasure in the fact that his works were being read, translated and performed as never before, not only in Scandinavia and the German-speaking world, but also in France, England and America. Shortly after, he made his breakthrough in Russia and the other Slav countries. As he approached his sixtieth birthday, books were written about him, both at home and

55 Henrik Ibsen in the year of his sixtieth birthday. Detail from Walther Firles' painting of 1888. The following summer he met Emilie Bardach – 'the May sun in a September life'.

abroad, and he was acclaimed, decorated and honoured as
never before. Twenty-seven years earlier he had more or less
fled the country; when at last he returned home, it was as
a world famous man. As he said in a letter to Hegel in
1892, he could now 'experience daily that I have both the
conservative party and the party of the left on my side'.

It is, however, profoundly characteristic of the restlessness
of Ibsen's mind, and of his tendency to swing from one
extreme to the other, that it should be precisely at this
point that doubt about his calling and its value woke to new
life in him. As he wrote in 1895, 'there is, of course, a
certain satisfaction in winning so much acceptance in the
countries round about, but it does not bring me any
happiness, and in the end, what is it all worth?'

Questions from the works of his youth reappear again, but
in a new perspective: one's vocation or human happiness,
writing or life. However, it is no longer a question of the
way forward, but of the road that is already behind one, and
of the decisions that can never be remade. Furthermore, it
is not only a question of one's own happiness, but that of
others too, of the price and the sacrifices which the life's work
has demanded, and of relationship to society and fellow
human beings in general. These are the themes on which he
was to dwell in the plays which he was still to write. *The
Master Builder, Little Eyolf, John Gabriel Borkman* and *When We
Dead Awaken.*

The questions were brought into focus by certain personal
experiences, first and foremost his friendship with two young
women, Helene Raff and Emilie Bardach, in Gossensass in
the summer of 1889. The latter particularly – 'the May
sun in a September life' as he called her – aroused strong
feelings and a deep unease in him, and eventually he
broke off their correspondence abruptly for the sake of his
conscience. Both appealed to the writer in him. He studied
them, and there are undoubtedly elements of Emilie Bardach

56 The eighteen-year-old Emilie Bardach met Ibsen for the first time on 22 July 1889, the day after the inauguration of the *Ibsenplatz* in Gossensass. The poet had noticed her during the ceremony, and found her the next day sitting on a park bench outside the hotel. Ibsen was obviously infatuated, and considered leaving Susanna, but after some months back in Munich, he wrote to Emilie telling her that she must no longer try to write to him.

in Hedda Gabler, and of both of them in Hilde Wangel as we meet her in *The Master Builder*. Hilde also owes something to the young Norwegian pianist, Hildur Andersen, who became Ibsen's intimate friend in Christiania. These young women could occasionally make him feel that reality could be more beautiful than art, as he once said in a letter to Emilie Bardach.

Shortly after Ibsen arrived back in Norway, Knut Hamsun gave a series of lectures in which he violently assaulted the writers of the older generation, Ibsen in particular. Ibsen himself was sitting in the front row, and was thus obliged to hear that the genre which he had cultivated all his life gave no room for subtle portrayal of character, and that he himself was so uncomplicated that he could not achieve deeper psychological insights. To be attacked in this way, and particularly with such arguments, by a young genius such as Hamsun, was something that could well exacerbate the feeling that it had all been in vain, and that his own time was soon to be over – a feeling which a year later was given dramatic form in *The Master Builder*.

It was approximately at this time that the ideas of the writer and philosopher Friedrich Nietzsche were giving rise to much discussion in the Scandinavian countries. They stimulated a lively debate about great men and the morality of the common good. Nietzsche's 'Übermensch' and Brandes' view of great men as the source of culture must in many ways have appealed to the individualist in Ibsen, though at the same time the 'Übermensch' morality would have challenged the humanist and democrat in him. This conflict was to leave visible marks in his plays, particularly *The Master Builder* and *John Gabriel Borkman*.

The confrontation had been latent for a long time. In the works of his youth the calling had been sacred; all other considerations had to yield to it, and women in particular had either to be sacrificed or to take second place to the man's vocation. However, as early as in *Pillars of Society*, judgement is passed on the man who betrays love for the sake of his life's work, and in the plays which follow, one of the main themes is a woman's right to her own life and to life-tasks of her own. From *Ghosts* onwards the joy of life, the free and happy development of the self, is posited as the highest good. Whereas in *The Wild Duck* Gregers Werle's idealism is misguided and hostile to life, and whereas the aristocratic æsthete Hedda Gabler gropes blindly, genuine values are found in the warm, simple and ordinary people – the Ekdals, the Tesmans and Thea Elvsted.

57   In 1895 Erik Werenskiold did a series of portraits of Ibsen, among them this chalk drawing of a smiling Ibsen. For the tight-lipped poet *could* smile. The writer Jonas Lie has told of convivial evenings with Ibsen in Berchtesgaden; 'the more his good humour grew, the more he beamed and laughed and shone, till at last he sat there like a good, kind, talkative granny!'

The society in which Ibsen had always been involved, and to which he had now returned, had become different. The idea of vocation and the duty of the elect lay in the continuation of the ideology of the official class, and the demand for the freedom and rights of the individual and for personal integrity were in line with the bourgeois liberalism of the opposition. Now, however, it was 'the unprivileged majority' which was knocking on the door, and in Ibsen there emerged a new recognition of the rights and worth of all human beings. In 1871, he had written to Brandes that he had never had much sympathy for 'solidarity', while in 1888, in a letter to Oscar Nissen, he says that it is 'the working class' which is closest to his heart. Two years later he declared publicly that he was very interested in 'the social-democratic question', that he had acquainted himself with it, and that in his works he had 'in certain cases, and without consciously aiming to do so, come to the same conclusion as the social-democratic moral philosophers in their scholarly works'.

The reevaluation now involves the writer himself, and puts a question mark against his life's work and the attitudes from which it had originated. In none of the works of his old age does he paint his own portrait, but in contrast to the majority of plays from *A Doll's House* to *Hedda Gabler*, the main character is now always a man, and a man who stands in a very tense relation to a vocation which is related to the dramatist's own. He finds himself profoundly isolated, recognizes that death is approaching, but longs to redeem a wasted life. All these main characters live in marriages that are either unhappy or full of friction; all have in one way or another betrayed their love and their social responsibility, and all of them are forced by a woman to confront their own past. Often too they are set in relief by secondary characters who represent other and more positive values and attitudes to life – from the happy road-builder Borghejm in *Little Eyolf* to the robust bear-hunter Ulfhejm in *When We Dead Awaken*, from the humble clerk Foldal in *John Gabriel Borkman* to Mrs Wilton with her zest for life.

In this way the four plays have not only thematic similarities, but structural ones also. The retrospective technique is highly developed in all of them, and they are all short and concentrated, three of them having only three acts. As never before Ibsen reveals his ability to condense into 'one scene what it takes months and years to live through', as Edvard Brandes wrote of *The Master Builder*. Indeed, they are to such an extent retrospective that the German Ibsen scholar Kurt Wais has, with considerable justification, called

58   In 1890 the student Carl Størmer took a series of photographs of well known men and women in the centre of
Christiania. Here he has caught Ibsen in characteristic style,
crossing Egertorvert on a summer's day in 1894.

them elegies. The style and the tone also come close to that of
poetic prose. Ibsen warned against performing or interpret-
ing the plays symbolically – 'I do not seek symbols, I portray
people' – but the dialogue, stage setting and course of action
all acquire strong symbolic undertones. It is characteristic
that they all end in the open air, and that the last one
takes place entirely outside. As Wais puts it: from the
bourgeois microcosmos we are again led out into the macro-
cosmos which we recognize from the works of Ibsen's youth.
Man is again placed in relation to the sea and sky.

The Master Builder

The Master Builder has links with *The Lady from the Sea* in that Hilde, Dr Wangel's youngest daughter, turns up at Solness's house and sets the plot in motion. There is also a deeper relationship between the works. In both, fairytale motifs and legendary material play a considerable part, for while occult powers are ascribed to The Stranger by Ellida Wangel, Solness experiences them in himself as serving spirits which he cannot control. For him a wish counts as a fully-fledged deed, much as in *Peer Gynt*, and trolls, which were perhaps given a new lease of life by Jonas Lie's *Trold* (1891-92), cause almost as much havoc in the mind of the master builder as they do in the Troll King's hall.

The master builder, Solness, is an artist in relation to his work. He has worked his own way up and now stands at the height of his powers. However, he fears that a reversal of fortunes will soon overtake him. Once in the past he had pushed his own teacher, Knut Brovik, ruthlessly aside, and now he is trying by all the means at his disposal to hold Brovik's son, Ragnar, down, precisely because he knows he is young and talented, and because he fears that 'retribution will come at the hands of youth'. One of the means he uses is the erotic-hypnotic influence he has over Kaja Fosli, Ragnar's fiancee.

Youth really does come knocking at the door, in the shape of Hilde Wangel, fresh from the mountains. She has come, not to depose him, but to demand that he fulfill a promise he once made, 'my kingdom on the table!' A rich and powerfully orchestrated relationship develops between them, carried and inspired by eroticism. She on her side has youth's demanding courage to live, he the sudden but anxious flare-up of the ageing man's thirst for life. He exposes all his wounds, his 'sick conscience', his 'dizziness', his deep feeling of guilt in relation to Aline. She has had to pay for his

59   Solness (August Oddvar) between the young woman
Hilde Wangel (Liv Strømsted Dommersnes) – who wants the
master builder himself to climb up and place the wreath on his
own building – and his anxious wife Aline, who says, 'you
know you cannot bear even to go out on to the second-floor
balcony'. Scene from Act II of the Norwegian National Theatre
production in 1950.

success with all that she had: the life of her children, and
her own vocation as a master builder, which was her ability
to build up the souls of the young, 'so that they might
grow straight and fine, and beautifully formed'. The same
fire which cleared the ground for him, laid her life waste
and transformed her into a living corpse. Although he had
not started the fire, he had desired it, and the wish makes
him guilty. He had 'luck on his side':

> But let me tell you what that sort of luck feels like! It
> feels like a great raw spot here in my breast. And these
> helpers and servants go flaying bits of flesh off other people

in order to close my wound. But the wound will never
heal ... never!

Later he understood that it was God who let this happen,
who took from him love and happiness so that he should
consecrate all his energies to the building of churches. However, he would not serve such a god, and so he did 'the
impossible', climbed the steeple at Lysanger and placed the
wreath on it himself, and then declared himself free from
the service of 'the Mighty One'. He refused to build churches
any more, only houses for people, happy homes, such as he
could never have.

Hilde takes up the struggle against his sick conscience, sets
her youth and confidence against his fear of retribution, and
arouses new hope and longings in him. Now he sees that
building houses for people is not worth twopence, and feels
that the whole of his life's work has been a failure. Instead
he wants to build the only thing in which human happiness
may be contained, 'castles in the air with solid foundations
underneath'. To do this, however, he must first repeat 'the
impossible', climb up the tower and place the wreath on it
himself, and then again declare himself free from the service
of 'the Great and Mighty Lord'. He reaches the top, but is
overcome by dizziness. His guilt feelings and fear of retribution – or retribution itself? – hurl him headling into the
quarry. However, in death he has been triumphant, he has
repeated the deed of his youth, he has done 'the impossible',
and Hilde hears harps in the air.

The whole play builds up to the final climactic scene. It
has done so through small hints and suggestions, but first
and foremost through the great dialogues between Hilde and
Solness, which weave almost continuously through the whole
play. They have the writer's touch of genius, being at the
same time concentrated and free-flowing, teasing and serious;
they are lyrical-dramatic antiphons, in a supple and lively

60 Despite this, the master builder himself climbs up with the wreath. Hilde (Johanne Dybwad) points up to him. A moment later he falls and is killed. 'But he reached the top. And I heard harps in the air. My – my master builder', exclaims Hilde. Norwegian National Theatre 1910.

prose, between two people who come ever closer to each other, and together rise to new heights, while expectations and a secret restlessness build up until the decision ripens in the master builder to stake everything on one great test.

When the play first appeared, many construed it allegorically or symbolically, and it was interpreted in the most diverse ways. However, Edvard Brandes dismissed all symbolical interpretations, and Ibsen thanked him for having so strongly emphasized the characters' 'quality of being real people'. This does not mean that Ibsen wanted to confine them within a narrow realism, but on the contrary that he believed that the complex and irrational life of the soul was also part of reality.

Despite all his conflicts, his turbulent mind, his guilt, his fear and his longings, Solness is a totally convincing real person. There are many layers to him, from the self-confident master on the outside, to the inwardly weak man with a sensitive conscience, and it is precisely for this reason that he is so r thless in his self-defence until Hilde breaks through it and l berates that which he has repressed. The other characters are grouped round him, and all are marked by him. Aline lives entirely in the shadow of her husband and of the catastrophe which struck her, but she bears her burden with self-annihilating humility. It is only in a short meeting with Hilde that she gives us a moving glimpse of the unhappy and defenceless spirit which hides behind the black clad exterior and the everlasting talk of duty. In shining contrast there is Hilde, who for ten years – from when she was 13 till now that she is 23 – has lived on the strength of the overwhelming impression which the master builder once made on her. Only this can explain the fascinating play of contrasts which characterize her when she is with him: childish dreams and intuitive feminine knowledge, unshakable seriousness and – in the last scene – ecstatic joy.

To see him great means more than life to her. Yet she is not blind to other considerations; even though she does not have an ailing conscience, she does have kindness of heart. She is more than willing to take Solness from Aline – until she gets to know her; then she shrinks back, 'I can't hurt someone I *know*'.

Despite the psychological motivation and nuances, there are still many features in the dialogue, in the plot and in the main character himself which invite – indeed almost compel – one to make an allegorical interpretation. First and foremost this is true of the demand that the master builder should 'climb as high as he builds'. This idea imposes a considerable strain on a realistic interpretation even if one accepts it under the sway of the illusion, but it makes perfectly good sense if one construes it metaphorically and associates it with the writer himself. In the Solness who first built churches, then houses for people, and now wants to build 'castles in the air with firm foundations' the parallel with Ibsen is clear. As early as in the poem 'Building Plans' he had assumed the role of master builder within a similar symbolic framework (see p. 85), and in an interview five years after the play was written, he said that it was for this play that he had drawn most on himself.

It thus seems reasonable to regard *The Master Builder* as something of a confession in symbolical-allegorical form, and perhaps also as an expression in cipher of thanks and explanation to those Hildes he himself had met. We probably come closest to the writer in the deep sense of guilt and irredeemable debt, in the doubt about the value of his own work and in the dream of a new life. However, there is also something universal in all this, and there is no need to force the allegory, nor to draw other people into the pattern or set an equals sign between Solness and Ibsen. *The Master Builder* is a play about the dramatist himself, but independent of him, a play about art and life, about the meeting between age and youth, and about the dream of the impossible.

Little Eyolf

Alfred Allmers in *Little Eyolf* (1894) is not an artist, but a moral philosopher – a role which was not alien to the writer of *Brand*. He does not have much of Solness's vitality, but nor does he share his 'sick conscience'. He certainly has feelings of guilt, but up till now they have been well hidden behind his 'life's vocation', the great book on *Human Responsibility* on which he has been working. In relation to Rita, his wife, he is weak and evasive, whereas she is 'a warm-blooded human being', earthy and spirited. Like Hedda she comes from an aristocratic background, and makes great demands of life and happiness, but in contrast to her, she can also make use of opportunities, and receive from others. In her healthy sensuality, she is without parallel in the works of Ibsen. But she can also be dangerous if rejected.

Little Eyolf, their only child, is the visible evidence of the disharmony in their marriage. He is 'lame in the leg' – like Peer's offspring by The Woman in Green – and the disablement is a result of a desperate sexual struggle between the parents. There is both symbolic and psychological motivation behind the child's fascination for The Rat Wife – 'do the master and mistress have anything gnawing in the house?' – and behind the fact that he 'slips out quietly and unnoticed' and follows her. Eyolf is only on the stage for a short while, but he is at the centre of the conflict the whole time. It is his death which provokes the great confrontation between his parents, which does not end until everything has been explained and the ground cleared. They cling to their sorrow, dwell on details, and hurl bitter accusations at each other. But it becomes evident that they are filled not so much with sorrow as with remorse and despair, for neither of them has felt any real love for the boy. Eventually too Allmers

has to admit that he has not loved Rita wholly and un-
dividedly either, but has been tempted by 'gold and green
forests' because he had his 'half-sister' Asta to take into
consideration, she whom he secretly called Little Eyolf. That
the boy became a cripple and drowned, now seems to them
to have been retribution for the fact that Allmers married
Rita for the sake of Asta.

Without knowing it, Allmers also betrayed his real love
that time, for it was Asta whom he loved. When he now asks
her to resume their old brother and sister relationship, she is
forced to tell him what she now knows: that they are not half
brother and sister. They realize too that they would have
been 'the right travelling companions' for each other. It is
not stated, but it seems fair to assume that his life's work
also would have stood a better chance at her side. Now all
is too late, irremediable. Asta flees both from him and from
herself, but follows the road-builder, Borghejm, who in all
respects is the positive counterpart to Allmers: happy and
cheerful, with an understanding of a child's needs, generous in
love, and without the least faith in 'the law of change' which
Allmers hides behind.

However, it is precisely when Rita and Allmers hit rock
bottom that this concept acquires new meaning. Rita feels
'very painfully' that a transformation is taking place in her,
but with it 'the loss of a whole life's happiness'. Allmers
replies – and it sounds like an echo from *Brand* – 'in that
loss is our gain'. Rita rejects the idea, 'empty phrases! Good
lord, when all is said and done we are still earthly creatures',
to which Allmers replies, 'yes, but related to the sea and
sky, also, Rita. (...) And *you* more than you know'. It is
furthermore the 'earthly creature', Rita, who first sees a new
possibility for them, a new life-task, that of taking into their
house the poor children from the waterfront.

There is great solemnity in the final scene. The flag is
hoisted and Allmers speaks – in the words of Wergeland – of

'the visitation of the spirits', while they both agree to turn their gaze 'upwards, towards the mountain peaks. Towards the stars. Towards the great silence'. To judge by what is said, it would seem that Ibsen wants us to believe in the transformation: that Rita has found a substitute for her lost happiness, and that with her Allmers will carry out his 'human responsibility' instead of writing about it. As in *The Lady from the Sea*, the solution lies on the ethical plane, and in contrast to Solness, who no longer wants to build houses for people, Rita and Allmers have woken up to their social responsibility.

But does the transformation go deep enough? Ibsen himself is said to have doubted that it was more than a passing mood in Rita. And what about Allmers? He has hidden deception and self-deception behind great resolves and big words before, and there are critics – especially the American, H. J. Weigand – who are of the opinion that he is doing so here too. The happy ending is not sufficiently grounded in the character portrayal. The whole work could – as Weigand believes – be a piece of bitter irony on the part of the writer. It could also be artistic weakness.

The play has neither the lyrical intimacy, nor the dramatic grandeur of *The Master Builder*, though there are many fine details. In a few lines it paints a masterly child portrait, while the Rat Wife is a superlative, fantastic creation, and the psychological analysis of Allmers a penetrating study of repression and 'vicarious motivation'.

John Gabriel Borkman

As a dramatic master builder, Ibsen was at the height of his power again in *John Gabriel Borkman* (1896), one of the most integrated and powerful plays he ever wrote. The outer drama, and particularly the antecedent history, resembles that of *Pillars of Society*, but it has far greater concentration and grandeur, and the character portrayal is far richer. The play revolves round one main character of grand dimensions in his potential for both good and evil, and centres on the betrayal of love, which here is far more deeply motivated psychologically and thematically, and has far more fateful consequences both inwardly and outwardly.

The unity of time is observed more strictly than ever before, the four acts following one right after the other, so that the dramatic time is no longer than the time it would take to perform the play without intermissions. The setting changes from act to act and in the middle of the final act, as dictated by the needs of the action. However, it also serves as a characteristic framework for the individuals involved – Mrs Borkman in her shabby sitting room, Borkman in the 'former great hall', furnished strictly in Empire style –, and as a mood-creating and symbolic background for the various phases of the dramatic development. Winter with its cold, its driving snow, deep drifts and pale moonlight dominates everything; and together winter in nature and in the hearts of men make up an overall picture, which with some justification Edvard Munch has called 'the most powerful snowscape in the whole of Scandinavian art'.

The characters stand in sharp relief against each other, both in their conflicts and in the light they shed on each other: sister against sister, woman against man, young against old. Borkman too stands between two women – and against them both: Gunhild his wife, and Ella Rentheim whom he once betrayed. The women are sisters – as in *The Feast at Solhoug* and *Pillars of Society* – twin sisters, moreover, and they have strong resemblances behind their widely differing facial features, which reflect their different fates, personalities and attitudes. Between them and against them stands Erhart, Borkman's son, who in his revolt against being guarded over, reveals something of his father's will. However, his lack of independence and his thirst for an unreflecting enjoyment of life stand in sharp contrast to his father's austere mining temperament. In the same way, both his demanding mother and his self-sacrificing foster mother are set in relief by his warm-blooded and somewhat frivolous fiancée, Mrs Wilton. Finally Borkman has both a parallel and an opposite in the clerk, Foldal, with his humble spirit and his dreams of becoming a writer.

In *Little Eyolf* the confrontation with the past dominated at the expense of the action on the present plane. In *John Gabriel Borkman* there is balance, while at the same time the two planes are intimately connected and are constantly intersecting each other. The bitter struggle concerning Erhart takes place totally in the present, starting at the beginning of the first act and continuing to the end of the third. In Act I the struggle between Ella Rentheim and Mrs Borkman is about him, but already Borkman is invisibly present, in the consequences of the catastrophe which he has brought on them all, but first and foremost in the bitterness and hatred which exists between the sisters; 'You and I, Gunhild, we have fought tooth and nail over a man before'. We hear him walking backwards and forwards in the room overhead, and in the second act we meet him in person in the midst of his overweening pride and un-fathomable loneliness, but with all his past around him, his old dreams and plans, his vision of greatness, his self-righteous bitterness, his expectations of restitution – and his secret doubts. It is here too that Ella Rentheim confronts him with the sin which he once committed against her. She makes demands on him concerning the here and now and draws him into the battle about Erhart, who in the third act is again the focal point, but who then tears himself free from them all in order to live his own life. Through all this Borkman is forced to stop living his sealed-off life in the past; he will now try to see if he can 'find his way to freedom and life and humanity again'. First, however, he wants to inspect all his 'hidden treasures', his dreams and

61   Gunhild Borkman (Ella Hval), Borkman (August Oddvar) and Ella Rentheim (Tore Segelcke) in a scene from the third act of *John Gabriel Borkman* at the Norwegian National Theatre in 1954. Mrs Borkman: 'what does he want down here?', Ella Rentheim: 'he wants to try to reach an under-standing with you, Gunhild'.

visions; he makes his way up to the look-out point as in his youth, and with Ella at his side – as then – he relives them in the final moments of his life. The play closes with a single monumental tableau: the two sisters who have always fought over him, and who each in their own way have been destroyed by him, can at last hold out their hands to each other, 'we two shadows – over the dead man'.

John Gabriel Borkman is one of the greatest dreamers in Ibsen's world, on a par with Brand, Peer and Julian. His dreams, though, are of a different kind: they have most in common with Peer's Sahara fantasies, but are more realistically based; they belong to the dawn of the age of industrial capitalism. He was a 'miner's son', and as a boy he heard the ore sing with joy when it was broken free, because it wanted to 'come up to the light of day and serve mankind'. It was this belief that was his starting point, the one he talked about to Ella when he was young, and it still forms part of his dying vision: it was wealth and happiness for men that he wanted to create. However, it soon came to be associated with the desire for power and money,

> I wanted to make all the sources of power in this land subservient to me. Everything that earth, mountain and forest contained of wealth, I wanted to subjugate. I wanted to create an empire for myself, and thereby prosperity for many thousands of others.

In order to become bank manager he betrayed Ella and married her sister, and it seems that from then on power, wealth and honour became his main objective. He worked his way up in the world, became a real Jon Gynt on a national scale, and misappropriated millions that had been entrusted to him – always in the belief that he belonged to 'the chosen'. Yet it is not this, but Ella's accusation which carries the most weight: when he betrayed her, he became guilty of what she in the great scene of confrontation calls 'the great sin for which there is no forgiveness (...) the sin of murdering the ability to love in a human being'. It was a double murder, 'the murder of your own soul and of mine!' Everything that has happened since can be traced back to that.

Borkman does not recognize any guilt. When at the end he looks out over the 'dreamland' he once shared with her, sees all the activity he should have set in motion and feels the veins of metal ore reaching out to him, he confesses his love of the 'life-craving treasures' deep in the earth – and deifies himself by his choice of words, 'for the kingdom ... and the power ... and the glory (...)'. It is then that Ella pronounces judgement over him, 'you will never win the prize you claimed for this murder. You will never make your triumphant entry into your cold, dark kingdom!' A moment later a 'hand of ice' – or 'a hand of iron' – clutches at his heart. Together the sisters sum up the results of his life: the cold 'had killed him long ago (...) One dead man and two shadows – that is what the cold has done. (...) Yes, the coldness of heart'.

Never had any Ibsen drama pronounced a more unambiguous and unconditional judgement, and the judgement falls on him who set dreams, a life-task, power and glory above love and living reality. His vision and philanthropic aims give him tragic dimensions, but they do not exonerate him. Furthermore the whole play supports the judgement, for he was to blame for a marriage which in its chilling horror matches those Strindberg described in *The Father* and *The Dance of Death*. Gunhild, who is always cold, he has disappointed and offended so deeply that she hates him, and sees in their son only an avenger for herself and the things that are hers. Erhart has always been a stranger to his father. Foldal is another of his innocent victims, and beyond him we glimpse countless others. Ella Rentheim lost all 'human happiness' from the day Borkman betrayed her; even the joy which comes from doing good disappeared. But his betrayal of her also rebounded on to Borkman himself, for she would have borne defeat and shame with him, and helped him to get on his feet again. Or maybe he would not have committed his crime if he had been true to her. In any case, his betrayal of faith to Ella was also fateful for the life-task to which he sacrificed her.

That Borkman was 'a miner's son' was a touch that was not added until the final draft, but via the poem 'The Miner' the words indicate a connection between the main character and the writer. It was a connection which Ibsen was to underline even more strongly in the work which was to be his last.

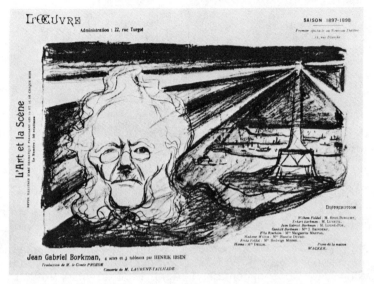

62   Edvard Munch's theatre poster for *John Gabriel Borkman* at the Noveau Theatre in Paris on the 8th and 9th of November 1897. The performance was preceded by a lecture, given by the French writer and anarchist, Laurent Tailhade.

When We Dead Awaken – A Dramatic Epilogue

Since *Pillars of Society*, there had never passed more than two years between Ibsen's plays, and shortly after *John Gabriel Borkman* had appeared, he had begun as usual to think about the next one. However, he was interrupted, for his German publisher suggested that he should prepare an edition of all he had written, and in 1898 his *Collected Works* appeared in both German and Norwegian. In the foreword to the Norwegian edition he emphasizes the inner continuity of his work: 'it is only by understanding and familiarizing oneself with my entire output as a coherent and continuous whole that the reader will receive the precise impression I sought to convey in the individual parts'. The old plan of writing an autobiography also woke to new life, and Ibsen

63   'A power of the first order'. Drawing in the Danish satirical newspaper *Blækspruten* (*The Octopus*), after the celebration dinner in Copenhagen on 1 April 1898 to mark Ibsen's seventieth birthday. The dinner had been something of a fiasco, apart from anything else because the main speaker did not turn up, and Professor Peter Hansen improvised a speech which was not particularly successful. He characterized Ibsen as 'a power of the first order', and the paper is here making fun of the situation. Sophus Schandorf, who can be seen behind Ibsen, was not successful with his speech either. Between the two unfortunates can be seen the minister of culture, Bishop Sthyr, and to the extreme right, Alexander Kielland, who is angry on behalf of his fellow countryman.

mentioned it in a speech he gave on his seventieth birthday, 'a book which will bring my life and my work together in an explanatory whole'. But this time too the plan was set aside, and a year later *When We Dead Awaken – A Dramatic Epilogue in Three Acts* appeared before the public.

In the summer of 1898, Ibsen said to William Archer, 'I have put the characters out to grass. I hope they will prosper'. So it seems that in the new play also the portrayal of people was to be the most important element, and that the writer would respect the protagonists' own lives and autonomy. The drafts show that he did so: in the finished play they do not behave in the way the writer had originally imagined. There is also a continuation of the compositional tautness from *John Gabriel Borkman*, and the use of symbolism is more marked than at any time since *Peer Gynt*. In *When We Dead Awaken*, Ibsen achieves the height of symmetrical simplicity of structure and character grouping, the maximum stylization in the portrayal of secondary figures, and a unique fusion of symbolism and realism.

Both in fact and symbolically, the action moves upwards from act to act, from the coastal resort in the first, via a 'vast, barren plateau' in the second, to 'a wild, precipitous place high in the mountains' in the third, and both weather and landscape correspond to what is going on in and between the individuals involved. The number of characters is small, but in temperament and appearance they form strongly marked contrasts, Rubek against Ulfhejm, Irene against Maja, but also Rubek against Maja, and Irene against Ulfhejm. The relationships between the couples, Rubek and Irene, Ulfhejm and Maja, run parallel too, in a way which highlights the contrasts and the central theme: art versus life. The scenes succeed one another in an equally simple pattern, but are joined together with the aid of recurring motifs, symbols, words and images.

The architecture of the play is austere, but no play by Ibsen is so rich in lyrical prose and elegaic moods – particularly in the second act, with its long, retrospective dialogues between Irene and Rubek. Yet despite the simple structure, the main characters and 'the meaning' of the play are as complex as ever.

The sculptor, Rubek, is the first main character since Falk who is an artist by profession, and his relation to Irene reminds one of Falk's to Svanhild. Irene, though, did not go off to a life 'of quiet duty': she was so profoundly offended in her nature as a woman that she 'died' of the fact that Rubek never touched her, but let her go when he no longer needed her for his work. When she meets him again, she is like a living corpse, constantly followed by a nursing sister with a straitjacket. She tells of her past in ambiguous, sinister words and images, calls him to account for her wasted, unhappy life, but at the same time asks about 'the child', the great sculpture for which she was the model. He tries to defend himself. It was his life's masterpiece he wanted to create, 'The Day of Resurrection', presented 'in the form of a young woman who wakes from the sleep of death – (...) She who wakes up was to be the world's noblest, purest, and most ideal woman. Then I found you (...)'. That he never touched her was partly because for him she became 'a sacred being', but also because he was filled with the 'superstition' that if he touched her or desired her, 'my mind would be profaned, so that I would not be able to create that which I was striving for. And I still believe there is some truth in that.'

What would have happened is an open question. Irene's attitude is ambivalent. She says she would have killed him on the spot; at the same time she accuses him and mocks him, 'first the work of art ... then the human being'. One thing, however, is certain, and that is that after Irene left him, his real work also came to an end, 'I have not written anything since that day. Only pottered and made models', because it was she who had the key to the casket which contained his visions. What he created later, made him world famous, but to him it meant nothing. Indeed, 'all this business about the artist's calling and the artist's mission began to seem to me so empty and hollow and meaningless'.

Of decisive importance is what happened to 'The Day of Resurrection' after Irene left him. She forces the confession out of him: the work was altered. A place had to be made for everything Rubek saw in the world about him, the vision

64 The sculptor Rubek (Stein Grieg Halvorsen) and Irene (Aase Bye) in a scene from the third act of *When We Dead Awaken* at the Norwegian National Theatre in 1961.

had to yield to the randomness of reality, and the figure of Irene got pushed to one side, its 'radiance of the light of joy' subdued.

This confession is the turning point of the drama. Irene whispers 'now you have pronounced judgement upon your-self', and is on the point of plunging the knife into him. She is not appeased by the fact that he has placed himself in the foreground as 'a man weighed down by guilt', 'remorse for a misspent life'. 'Poet!' she says, hard and cold, and she explains, 'because you are weak and spineless and full of forgiveness for all you have done and thought'. He himself acknowledges his weakness, 'for you see, I was born to be an artist – and so can never be anything else but an artist'. When she again calls him a poet, it is because 'there's something exonerating in that word, my friend. Something which forgives all sins, which draws a veil over all weakness'.

However, her accusations break through with renewed strength because he has betrayed their 'child'. This has made her guilty too, for she was a human being of flesh and blood with a destiny to fulfill, that of giving birth to real, living children. They recall their poetic happiness while the work was in progress, and while they do so the wish 'to live life over again' grows in Rubek. Irene knows it is impossible, 'when we dead awaken', – 'what do we see then?', 'we see that we have never lived'. Even so they dare to set out for the mountain peak despite Ulfhejm's warning, and Irene's recognition that 'the love which belongs to our earthly life – our glorious, wonderful life on earth – our mysterious life – that is dead in both of us'. They want 'to live life to the full once more' before they go down into their graves again. They climb towards the 'promised peak' to celebrate their wedding feast, but rolling mists 'settle densely over the land-scape', and while Maja, rejoicing, returns to the freedom of the valley with the bear-hunter, Irene and Rubek – like Brand – are overtaken by an avalanche and buried in the snow. But here there is no question, and no answer. The nun proclaims peace over the dead.

The attempt was doomed to fail. A wasted life cannot be lived over again. No resurrection follows in its wake. That which was possible in *Little Eyolf*, and probable in *John Gabriel Borkman*, is here the main point: the betrayal of life and love destroy the work also. Rubek violated both life and art and is therefore pronounced a murderer. In one of his recurrent replies he even assigns himself the role of the tempter in the desert. Despite this, he has more redeeming

features than Allmers or Borkman; there was nothing cal-
culating behind his betrayal, but rather a feeling of deep
commitment. Like Solness, he looks his guilt and his loss in
the face, and he is tragically destroyed in an attempt to
restore what was lost, to realize the impossible.

When We Dead Awaken is a play about art and life, more
particularly about the artist's ambivalent and conflict-ridden
relationship to both. The profoundly personal involvement
in the play is evident from many of its spoken lines and
the sculptor is even referred to as a poet. The fact too that
in the final version Ibsen changed the word 'play' in the
subtitle to 'epilogue' means that he ascribed to it a special
place in his output, a personal address to the public. At the
time it was understood as a final commentary on the
authorship as a whole, but that is not how it was intended.
In an interview, Ibsen himself said that it was an epilogue
to the series of plays which began with *A Doll's House*. Though
whether he intended it as a farewell to the realistic form, as
a recognition and explanation of the scepticism and mis-
anthropy which had gained ground after the noble figure
of Nora, or whether he had something quite different in
mind – that is something we shall never know.

The play draws together themes and motifs which go much
farther back, not only, as we have already seen, to *Brand*
and *Love's Comedy*, but also to the mountain and valley
symbolism of 'On the Heights', and to *Emperor and Galilean*;
for beyond the opposites of art and life, and Irene and Rubek
on the one hand, and Maja and Ulfhejm on the other, we
again glimpse the dream of a synthesis. Most striking,
however, are the elements which link Irene with Furia in
Ibsen's very first play: they have both been shut in, and they
both call themselves 'dead', and Furia's dagger, furthermore,
corresponds to Irene's stiletto. There are also more important
common features behind these external similarities. Both
women are intimately connected with the hero's conscious-

ness of his vocation, and at the same time pursue him with their love-hate. They are evidence of the deep ambivalence which the poet felt in relation to his calling.

In the end the tragedy of Rubek and Irene became an epilogue to the whole authorship, a moving and poetic confession about the struggle and the sacrifices which were demanded of a writer who dreamt of 'the wonderful life on earth', but who 'was born an artist'.

On his seventieth birthday Ibsen said that he still had 'various bits of madness in store', and two years later he wrote that if his strength held he would probably not be able to stay away from the old battlefields in the long run. 'But if I do appear there again, it will be with new weapons and new armour.' A few days later he suffered his first stroke, and a year later another one, after which he could no longer work. He died on 23 May 1906.

'– the Rome of modern drama'

Ibsen's authorship stretches over half a century, but it is of one piece from beginning to end. Through all his works we can trace the same basic themes in ever changing patterns and combinations. Certain types of personality, groupings and motifs have a marked tendency to reappear again and again, but in ever new surroundings. Ibsen's unique artistic hallmark remains in many ways nearly the same throughout his entire production, even though the quality of the works may vary greatly. His hallmark is a basically tragic mood with an element of mystical fatalism, a lively feeling for character and conflict, for development and psychological motivation, for undertones and hidden associations, scenic grouping, suggestive visual images and significant dialogue.

It has also been shown how the authorship constantly renewed itself with regard to vision and attitude, technique and subject matter. The dramatist was constantly seeing his themes in a new light, trying them out in new characters and constellations. His work resembles an ongoing inner dialogue about the vital issues of life, and it is this which makes his work not just a series of individual plays, but a self-contained whole, a moving drama in its own right.

The most important turning point is half way through, and it is closely associated with the play which Ibsen regarded as his main work. A romantic idealism is replaced by a critical-analytical realism in life as well as in dramatic form. The dividing line is not absolute: it is anticipated in the preceding works, and elements of a romantic and religious-idealistic inspiration and philosophy of life continue to the end. There are also important dividing lines within each main section: in the first, the break with national roman-ticism, and in the second, the shift of emphasis from social and critical realism to psychological analysis and a more symbolic realism, which ends in the late self-questioning works.

The dramatist's attitude to his own work also changes. Time and again he emphasizes that everything he has written 'is intimately connected with what I have lived through in my imagination, even if I have not experienced it in reality'. It is in this letter from 1880 that he also quotes the lines, about 'holding / judgement day over oneself'. This con-nection between inner experience and art is most obvious in the first main phase and the very last. From 1870 onwards Ibsen asserts ever more strongly that the writer's prime task is to *see*, not to preach or philosophize. Even in the 1880s, when he shows a strong fighting spirit and urge to extend boundaries, he says that he stands totally outside his work, and in the 1890s he repeatedly emphasizes that his only aim has been the portrayal of character. In 1898 he says that he has no philosophy of his own, and does not think that he has ever preached 'a single truth'.

Despite this, his contemporaries regarded him, even in his later writings, as being primarily a preacher – a spokesman

65 'Henrik Ibsen in the World Theatre'. Caricature by Alfred Schmidt in *Hver 8. dag* (*Every Eighth Day*), on the occasion of Ibsen's seventieth birthday in 1898. Among the ruling monarchs in the stalls are, *inter alia*, Kaiser Wilhelm II, Queen Victoria and Emperor Frans Josef. In the balcony one can see Drachmann, Kielland, Strindberg, Lie, Bjørnson and other Scandinavian writers.

for philosophical, ethical, and to some extent also political truths. Many have found slogans in his work, and yet it is far from certain that such slogans express his own opinions. The plays tend to end in open questions, and the more one immerses oneself in them, the more difficult it becomes to extract a simple and unambiguous 'truth' out of them. At any rate, any 'message' we can find, lies less in certain utterances than in the works as artistic wholes, the internal relationship between them, and above all in the existential seriousness of which they are born, the questioning and critical approach, the unrelenting preoccupation with fundamental ethical, psychological and social problems, the desire for truth, the dearly bought faith in human dignity and potential, freedom and responsibility, that which gives a meaning to such words as betrayal, guilt and retribution.

To a large extent the changing phases of Ibsen's authorship correspond to the usual period divisions of Scandinavian and European literary history, from late romanticism and 'poetic realism', through realism and naturalism to neo-romanticism and symbolism. But he never became the slave of any of these movements. He broke away from romanticism, but never finished with it. He became a realist and even came close to naturalism, but his vision of man has a perspective – freedom and responsibility – which the strict naturalist would have to deny, and his austere dramatic form is irreconcilable with the naturalistic representation of reality. The use of symbols in his later works is in line with European symbolism and Scandinavian neo-romanticism, but these works too are borne up by an ethical and social consciousness which is alien to the typical symbolist and neo-romantic. Finally, when in the works of his old age he sets life and human responsibility against art, this is in diametric opposition to the cult of art which characterizes the symbolists and neo-romantics.

The major political events of the period also produced

changes in Ibsen's works, which stand in an intimate and conflict-ridden relationship to Norwegian class-society. The national-historical plays, which revolve round leadership and the idea of unity, are linked to the view which the official class had of itself in the 1850s and 1860s. But *Love's Comedy* mocks the bureaucratic life-style, and *Brand*, like *Peer Gynt* directs a blow at the glorification of the farmer, and presents a terrifying picture of emergent capitalism. *Emperor and Galilean* has a broader European background and is influenced by the dynamism which was a result of

66 Henrik Ibsen at his writing table in Arbiens Street in Christiania in 1898.

industrialization, the growth of middle classes and the beginnings of the labour movement. The belief in 'the spirit of truth and freedom' which is expressed in the earliest contemporary plays is in accord with the highest ideals of bourgeois liberalism. However, right from Bernick, through Helmer and the businessman Werle, to John Gabriel Borkman, Ibsen portrays pillars of society who in reality deny the liberal ideals; at the same time he portrays women and independent intellectuals who hold them high. Moreover, both the conflicts described and the image of society presented express a critical attitude to the whole capitalist system, in which human values such as truth, freedom and love are made into objects which can be bought and sold. *This* is the source of all misery in the majority of plays starting with *Pillars of Society*. Thus Ibsen exposes contradictions and distortions in society: at the same time his noblest characters have an ethical consciousness and desire for truth which gives hope for 'the ability of ideals to propagate themselves' and for their 'evolutionary capability'. He pinned his hopes more and more on the working class, though he hardly knew it. As a dramatist he stays close to the milieu and conflicts which had the deepest roots in himself, and to the individualistic and retrospective dramatic form, which he developed with such mastery.

As the Swedish literary scholar, Martin Lamm, says in his book on modern drama, 'Ibsenian drama is the Rome of modern drama; all roads lead to it and from it'. Among other things, he points out how Ibsen bridged the gap which had grown up between literary drama and the art of the theatre during the romantic era, when writers wrote 'reading dramas' and the theatres staged popular plays of intrigue. According to Lamm, the greatest contribution of Ibsen to literary history was perhaps his fusion of reading drama and theatrical drama.

Inspiration from many sources merge in Ibsen's historical plays: Shakespeare's imagery and knowledge of men, Schiller's and Oehlenschläger's intellectual conflicts and historical perspective, Scribe's intrigue technique, and Bjørnson's living prose. The powerful originality of the great dramatic poems also draws on many and rich sources. From the French bourgeois problem play he learns about technique and choice of subject matter, and from Hebbel's bourgeois tragedies, about possible types of conflict. As a result, and presumably under the influence of the great classical Greek dramatists, he creates the modern tragedies, which are his most original and significant contribution to world drama.

He finds his modern tragic hero and modern tragic conflict in the bourgeois individual – often a woman – who rebels against society and tradition. He develops a unique kind of dramatic realism, creates a pattern of dialogue which combines the ease of daily speech with dramatic pregnancy, and visual images which are at once close to everyday reality and rich in latent symbolism. He deepens the psychological, ethical and social analysis through his retrospective technique, while at the same time he gives the works concentration and grandeur and a powerful element of tragic guilt and fate akin to the Greek.

It is first and foremost from his modern bourgeois plays that the roads lead out into world drama, to countless imitators, but also to independent disciples. Strindberg, Gerhart Hauptmann and Eugene O'Neill went further along the naturalistic road before they each in their own way developed new forms. In England, Bernard Shaw saw Ibsen as the great critic of idealism, idolized him as an example for his own problem and discussion plays, and was followed by many more. The symbolists cherished the symbolic elements, while Anton Chekov was inspired by the tragi-comic melancholy of a work such as *The Wild Duck* (cf. *The Seagull*). In Gregers Werle and many of his later protagonists Ibsen has laid bare psychological motivation and human inadequacy to such an extent that he has rendered suspect the very type of hero he himself created. For this reason his contemporary plays mark not only the breakthrough and epitome of bourgeois drama, but also the turning point. And for the same reason they point directly or indirectly towards more recent tragi-comedies, plays without a hero, and perhaps too to the theatre of the absurd.

Ibsen has a place not only in the development of the drama, but also in the context of the history of ideas. Both his boundless individualism and his æstheticism originate in romanticism. Like so many of his contemporaries – among

67 The poet no longer writes, but continues to take a walk down Karl Johan. Carl Størmers photograph from 1899.

them Flaubert and Kierkegaard, Brandes and Tolstoi – he tried to free himself from æstheticism, but to his dying day he remained a pronounced individualist. His individualism was presumably strengthened by Kierkegaard, perhaps too by the anarchists, but was modified by Hegel's view of history, which provided a powerful impetus for his 'masterpiece'; it was challenged by Nietzsche, and perhaps counteracted by 'the social democratic moral philosophers' (see p. 169). Through all phases, however, and all possible or likely influences, the ethics of will and responsibility permeate his work, thus linking him to the existential tradition.

We do not know much about what Ibsen read, and what we know is incidental; many of the writers who may have provided him with inspiration are long forgotten names. But from a literary-historical point of view he is in line with the foremost novelists of the period, the great Russians – Turgenyev, Tolstoi, and more especially Dostoyevsky. As Edvard Brandes has already pointed out, Ibsen with his penetrating ethical and psychological analyses did the same within the framework of the drama as Dostoyevsky did within the framework of the novel. Among the writers who owe him much are not only dramatists, but also modern novelists such as James Joyce.

The controversy concerning Ibsen continued for a long time, and centred primarily on the moral and social – or immoral and socially destructive – ideas which were to be found in his plays. But the literary values were also called into question by, among others, Knut Hamsun. Later there followed almost unanimous recognition. Then critical voices could be heard again, among them, those of the Swedish writer Pär Lagerkvist and the German expressionists after World War I. They particularly attacked the realistic contemporary plays, and these were later depreciated by other critics, particularly in the English-speaking countries, who regarded them as dated and unpoetic. However, they have also been warmly defended on various premises. John Northam and Daniel Haakonsen have found poetic qualities in the midst of – or under – the realism, while still others have defended realism as being of value in itself. A few Marxist critics have branded Ibsen's works as the product of the bourgeois-liberal era, and as such, out of date, while others like Horst Bien in East Germany, are of the opinion that they point beyond their own time and society and directly or indirectly defend human values which only the future will be able to realize.

The debate shows no sign of coming to an end, and it is supported by research which began in Ibsen's lifetime, and which in the course of the years has thrown much new light on his work. The strongest evidence of the vitality of Ibsen's work, however, is the fact that many of them are continually being performed, and occasionally reinterpreted, in the theatres both of Scandinavia and the world. They have also shown themselves to be well suited for radio and television. It has been proved time and again that they appeal just as strongly to the broad theatre public as they do to critics, scholars and producers. That should be a safe guarantee of a long life.

Henrik Ibsen:
An English Language Bibliography
Compiled by Astrid Tørud

BIOGRAPHIES

ARCHER, WILLIAM:
Ibsen's apprenticeship – in *Fortnightly Review*, lxxv, 1904
– On Ibsen's period in Bergen 1851–57.

BULL, FRANCIS:
Ibsen, the man and the dramatist – Oxford, 1954. Repr.
in *Ibsen-Årbok* 1954.

DUE, CHR.:
Ibsen's early youth – in *The Critic*, New York, xlix, 1906.

GRUMMAN, PAUL HENRY:
Henrik Ibsen, an introduction to his life and works – New York,
1928.

HARDWICK, MICHAEL AND HARDWICK, MOLLIE:
Henrik Ibsen – in *Great Europeans: Builders of Western
Civilization* (ed. J. Canning). London, 1973.

HEIBERG, HANS:
Henrik Ibsen – trans. by V. Yakuba. Moscow, 1975.

IBSEN, BERGLIOT:
*The Three Ibsens: memories of Henrik, Suzannah and Sigurd
Ibsen* – trans. by G. Schjeldrup. London, 1951.

JÆGER, HENRIK:
The Life of Henrik Ibsen – trans. by Clara Bell. London,
1890.

KOHT, HALFDAN:
Life of Ibsen – trans. by Einar Haugen and A. E. Santani-
ello. New York, 1971.

MACFALL, HALDANE:
Ibsen, the man, his art and his significance – London, 1907.

MEYER, MICHAEL:
Henrik Ibsen. A Biography – 3 vols. London, 1967–70.
Vol. 1 The making of a Dramatist 1828–1864.
Vol. 2 The Farewell to Poetry 1864–1882.
Vol. 3 The Top of a Cold Mountain 1883–1906.
Also an abridged version by Penguin, Harmondsworth,
1974.
MONTROSE, J. MOSES:
Henrik Ibsen; the man and his plays – New York, 1908.

TRANSLATIONS

The Collected Works of Henrik Ibsen. (Copyright ed.) Trans.
and ed. by William Archer. London, 1906 – 12 vols.
The Oxford Ibsen. Edited by James Walter McFarlane.
Oxford, 1960–77 – 8 vols., with introductions to the plays,
commentaries and select bibliographies.
Everyman's Library: *Lady Inger of Ostraat, Love's Comedy, The
League of Youth.* Trans. by R. Farquharson Sharp, 1915;
Brand. Trans. by F. E. Garrett, with an introduction by
P. H. Wicksteed, 1915. New ed. with an introduction by
Brian W. Downs, 1961; *Peer Gynt.* Trans. R. Farquharson
Sharp, 1921; *The Pretenders, Pillars of Society, Rosmersholm.*
Trans. by R. Farquharson Sharp, 1913; *A Doll's House,
The Wild Duck, The Lady from the Sea.* Trans. by
R. Farquharson Sharp and E. Marx-Aveling, 1910; *Ghosts,
The Warriors at Helgeland, An Enemy of the People.* Trans. by
R. Farquharson Sharp, 1911; *Hedda Gabler, The Master
Builder, John Gabriel Borkman.* Trans. by Eva Le Gallienne
and Norman Ginsbury, with an introduction by Brian W.
Downs, 1966.
Penguin volumes: *Peer Gynt.* Trans. by Peter Watts, 1950;
*A Doll's House, and other plays (The League of Youth, The Lady
from the Sea).* Trans. by Peter Watts, 1950; *Ghosts, and
other plays (A Public Enemy, When We Dead Wake).* Trans.

by Peter Watts, 1950; *The Master Builder, and other plays* (*Rosmersholm, Little Eyolf, John Gabriel Borkman*). Trans. by Una Ellis-Fermor, 1950; *Hedda Gabler, and other plays* (*Pillars of the Community, The Wild Duck*). Trans. by Una Ellis-Fermor, 1950.

The Plays of Ibsen. Trans. by Michael Meyer. London, 1960: *The Pretenders, Brand, Peer Gynt, Pillars of Society, A Doll's House, Ghosts, An Enemy of the People, The Wild Duck, Rosmersholm, The Lady from the Sea, Hedda Gabler, The Master Builder, Little Eyolf, John Gabriel Borkman, When We Dead Awaken.*

Henrik Ibsen: Four Major Plays. Trans. and with a preface by Rolf Fjelde. New York, 1965, new ed. 1970. 2 vols. – Vol. 1: *A Doll's House, The Wild Duck, Hedda Gabler, The Master Builder;* Vol. 2: *Ghosts, An Enemy of the People, The Lady from the Sea, John Gabriel Borkman.*

Henrik Ibsen: Letters and Speeches. Ed. Evert Sprinchorn. New York, 1964, London, 1965.

Brand: A New Version. Trans. by Geoffrey Hill. London, 1978.

ANTHOLOGIES

Contemporary Approaches to Ibsen. (ed. Daniel Haakonsen) Proceedings of the international Ibsen Seminars. Oslo, Bergen, Tromsø U.P., no. 1 1965; no. 2 1971; no. 3 1976. (Referred to as *Cont. App.* in the bibliography, these volumes are identical with the *Ibsen-Årbok* of the same years.)

Discussions of Henrik Ibsen. (ed. James Walter McFarlane) Boston, 1962 – Essays by various hands.

Henrik Ibsen. Penguin critical anthology. (ed. James Walter McFarlane) London, 1970.

Ibsen. A collection of Critical Essays. (ed. Rolf Fjelde) New Jersey, 1965.

Ibsen-Årbok. (ed. Einar Østvedt) Oslo, Bergen, Tromsø, 1952 – The Annual Ibsen Yearbook.

IBSEN AND HIS RELATIONSHIP TO WORLD DRAMA

ARUP, JENS:
Narrative and Symbol in Ibsen – in *The Listener*, 1959.
Repr. in *Discussions of Henrik Ibsen*. (ed.) J. W. McFarlane.
Boston, 1962.

ANDERSEN, ANNETTE:
Ibsen in America – in *Scandinavian Studies and Notes*, 14,
1937.

ANDERSON, M. A.:
Norse Trolls and Ghosts in Ibsen – in *Journal of Popular
Culture*, Ohio, 1971.

ARCHER, WILLIAM:
The true greatness of Ibsen; a lecture delivered at UCL –
in *Edda*, xii, 1919.

ARESTAD, SVERRE:
The Ibsen hero – in *The Hero in Scandinavian Literature*.
(eds. J. M. Weinstock and R. T. Rovinsky) Texas UP,
1975 – concentrates attention on Brand, Peer Gynt, Mrs
Alving and Solness.

ARESTAD, SVERRE:
Ibsen's portrayal of the artist – in *Edda*, lx, June, 1960.

BENTLEY, ERIC:
The Playwright as a Thinker – New York, 1946.

BERMEL, A.:
Ordinary Characters: An Interpretation of the Modern Theatre –
New York, 1973.

BEYER, EDVARD:
Ibsen today – in *Ibsen Årbok*, 1971/72.

BOTTMAN, P. N.:
Ibsen's Apollonian-Dionysian Dialectic: a Reconsideration – in *Facets of Scandinavian Literature*, Lexington, 1974.

BOYESEN, H. H.:

A Commentary on the Works of Henrik Ibsen – London, 1894.

BRADBROOK, M. C.:

Ibsen and the Past Imperfect – in *Ibsen-Årbok*, 1970/71. (*Cont. App. 2*)

BRADBROOK, M. C.:

Ibsen the Norwegian – London, 1948. New ed. 1966 – On Ibsen's national background.

CAFFIN, CHARLES:

The appreciation of the Drama – New York, 1918.

CAMPBELL, T. M.:

Hebbel, Ibsen and the analytical exposition – Heidelberg, 1922.

COLUM, P.:

Ibsen in Irish writing – in *Irish Writing*, 1949.

CROMER, V.:

James and Ibsen – in *Contemporary Literature*, 25, 1973. Comparing Henrik Ibsen and Henry James.

DEER, I.:

Ibsen, precursor of the absurd – in *South Atlantic Modern Language Association*, Washington, 1970.

DENNIS, NIGEL:

Ibsen unchained – in *Encounter*, xiv, May, 1960. Repr. in *Dramatic Essays*.

DOWNS, BRIAN:

Ibsen. The Intellectual Background – Cambridge, 1946.

DOWNER, ALAN:

The Art of the Play – New York, 1955.

EGAN, M. (ed.):

Ibsen. The Critical Heritage – London, 1972. Introduction and list of translations of Ibsen's plays, and critical writings during the period 1872–1906.

EGAN, M.:

Henry James. The Ibsen Years – London, 1972. On the profound effect of Ibsen on Henry James.

ELLER, W. H.:
  Ibsen in Germany. 1870–1900 – Boston, 1918.
ELLIS-FERMOR, UNA:
  Ibsen and Shakespeare as Dramatic Artists – in *Edda,* 1956.
ERBE, BERIT:
  Actors' Problems at the Ibsen Premières – in *Ibsen-Årbok,* 1975/6. (*Cont. App. 3*)
EWBANK, INGA-STINA:
  Ibsen and 'The Far More Difficult Art' of prose – in *Ibsen-Årbok,* 1970/71. (*Cont. App. 2*) – On the language and style.
EWBANK, INGA-STINA:
  Ibsen's dramatic language as a link between his 'realism' and his 'symbolism' – in *Ibsen-Årbok,* 1965/66. (*Cont. App. 1*)

FJELDE, ROLF:
  The Dimensions of Ibsen's Dramatic World – in *Ibsen-Årbok,* 1970/71. (*Cont. App. 2*)
FRANC, MIRIAM A.:
  Ibsen in England – Boston, 1919.

GASSNER, JOHN:
  Masters of the Drama – New York, 1940.
GASSNER, JOHN:
  Form and Idea in Modern Theatre – New York, 1956.
GILMAN, RICHARD:
  Ibsen and Strindberg – in his *The Confusion of Realms* – New York, 1969.
GILMAN, R.:
  The Making of Modern Drama: A Study of Buchner, Ibsen . . . – New York, 1974.
GILMAN, R.:
  The Search for Ibsen – in his *Common and Uncommon Masks. Writings on Theatre 1961–1970* – New York, 1970. On Ibsen as a poetic writer.

GRABOWSKI, S.:

Unreality in Plays of Ibsen, Strindberg and Hamsun – in *Mosaic*, 4, Manitoba, 1970.

GREGERSEN, HALFDAN:

Ibsen and Spain – Cambridge, Mass., 1936.

HAUGEN, EINAR:

Ibsen in America – in *Edda*, lvi, 1956.

HAUGEN, EINAR:

The living Ibsen – in *Quarterly Journal of Speech*, XLI, 1955.

HELLER, OTTO:

Henrik Ibsen; plays and problems – New York, 1912.

HENN, T. R.:

A Note on Ibsen – in his *The Harvest of Tragedy* – London, 1956.

JORGENSON, THEODORE:

Henrik Ibsen; a study in art and personality – Minnesota, 1945.

JOYCE, JAMES:

Ibsen's new drama – in *Fortnightly Review*, 73, 1900. Also in *Discussions of Henrik Ibsen.* (ed.) J. W. McFarlane. Boston, 1962.

KAUFMANN, F. W.:

Ibsen's Concept of Truth – in *Germanic Review*, xxxii, 1957.

KNUDSEN, TRYGVE:

Phases of Style and Language in the Works of Henrik Ibsen – in his *Skrifttradisjon og litteraturmål* – Oslo, 1967.

KOHT, HALVDAN:

Shakespeare and Ibsen – in *Journal of English and Germanic Philol.*, XLIV, 1945. Also in *Ibsen. A Collection of Critical Essays.* (ed. R. Fjelde) New Jersey, 1965.

LAVRIN, JANKO:

Ibsen and his creation – London, 1921.

LAVRIN, JANKO:

Ibsen: an approach – London, 1950.

LUCAS, F. L.:
The Drama of Ibsen and Strindberg – London, 1962.

McDONALD, J.:
The actors' contribution to early Ibsen; performances in London, 1889–97 – in *Scandinavia*, 15, 1975.

McFARLANE, JAMES WALTER:
Ibsen and the Temper of Norwegian Literature – London, 1960.

MAGOUN, F. P.:
Ibsen: Women's votes and women's lib. – in *Neuphilologische Mitteilungen*, 74.

MORI, MITSUYA:
Ibsen in Japan since 1970 – in *Ibsen-Årbok*, 1975/76. (*Cont.* App. 3)

MORRIS, W. D.:
Ibsen and ethics of self-realization – in *Germanic Notes*, 5, 1974.

NILSSON, NILS ÅKE:
Ibsen in Russland – Stockholm, 1958.

NORTHAM, JOHN:
Ibsen – Romantic, Realist or Symbolist? – in *Isben-Årbok*, 1975/76 (*Cont. App. 3*)

PEACOCK, RONALD:
The Poet and the Theatre – London, 1946.

POPPERWELL, RONALD:
Ibsen in the United Kingdom 1970–1975 – in *Ibsen-Årbok*, 1975/76. (*Cont. App. 3*)

REINERT, OTTO:
Ibsen and the Modern tradition – in *Ibsen-Årbok*, 1974.

ROBERTS, R. ELLIS:
Henrik Ibsen; a critical study – London, 1912.

ROSE HENRY:
Henrik Ibsen; poet, mystic and moralist – London, 1913.

SETTERQUIST, JAN:
Ibsen and the Beginning of Anglo-Irish Drama – Uppsala, 1951.

SHAW, GEORGE BERNARD:
   The Quintessence of Ibsenism – London, 1891. New ed. 1913.
SMIDT, K.:
   T. S. Eliot, William Archer, and Henrik Ibsen – in his
   The Importance of Recognition: Six Chapters on T. S. Eliot –
   Tromsø, 1973. Repr. in *Americana Norvegica* 4.
SPEER, J. H.:
   The Rhetoric of Ibsenism: a Study of the Poet-as-
   Persuader – in *Southern Speech Communication Journal* –
   Georgia, 37, 1972.
STEINER, GEORGE:
   The Death of Tragedy – New York/London, 1961.
STEWART, K.:
   Maurice Guest and the siren voices – in *Australian Lit.
   Studies*, 5, 1974.
STOLL, E. E.:
   Poets and Playwrights – Minneapolis, 1930 – On Ibsen and
   Shakespeare.
SUVIN, D.:
   Modes of political drama – in *Massachusetts Review*, 13,
   1974.

TENNANT, P. F. D.:
   Ibsen's Dramatic Technique – Cambridge, 1948.
THOMPSON, ALAN R.:
   The Anatomy of Drama, Berkely, 1942 and later eds.
TOSHIHIKO, SATO:
   Henrik Ibsen in Japan – in *Edda VLXII, 1962* – On Ibsen's
   influence on the modern Japanese dramatic movement.
TURCO, A. JR.:
   Ibsen, Wagner and Shaw's changing view of Idealism – in
   The Shaw Review, 17, 1974.
TYSDAHL, B. J.:
   Byron, Norway and Ibsen's *Peer Gynt* – in *English Studies*,
   Amsterdam, 56, 1975.

TYSDAHL, B. J.:
Joyce and Ibsen – A study in Literary Influence – Oslo, New York, 1968.

VALENCY, MAURICE:
The Flower and the Castle. An Introduction to Modern Drama – New York/London, 1963 – On Ibsen and Strindberg.

WAAL, C.:
Rhetoric in Action: Orators in the Plays of Henrik Ibsen – in *Southern Speech Communication Journal*, Georgia, 37, 1972.

WALL, J.:
Ibsen and Kierkegaard – in *Theatre Research*, 13.

WILLIAMS, RAYMOND:
Henrik Ibsen – in his *Drama from Ibsen to Eliot* – London, 1952. Rev. ed. 1964.

WILLIAMS, RAYMOND:
Ibsen's non-Theatrical Plays – in *The Listener*, 1949. Repr. in his *Drama from Ibsen to Eliot* (see above). Also repr. in *Ibsen-Årbok*, 1960/62. Also repr. in *Discussions of Henrik Ibsen*. (ed. J. W. McFarlane) Boston, 1962.

WILSON, KNIGHT G.:
Ibsen – Edinburgh, 1962.

ZANONI (PSEUD.):
Ibsen and the Drama – London, (1894 ?).

ZENTNER, JULES:
Ibsen's new Visibility in America – in *Ibsen-Årbok*, 1975/76. (*Cont. App. 3*)

CRITICAL WORKS ON THE PLAYS OF HENRIK IBSEN

ADLER, J. H.:
Two Hamlet Plays: *The Wild Duck* and *The Sea Gull* – in *Journal of Modern Literature*, Philadelphia, 1970 – On *The Wild Duck*, comparing it with *Hamlet*.

ANDERSON, A. R.:

Ibsen and the classical world – in *The Classical Journal*, xi, 1916 – On *Catiline*.

ARESTAD, SVERRE:

Ibsen's concept of tragedy – in *Publications of the Modern Language Association of America*, lxxiv, June, 1959 – On Ibsen's concept of tragedy through an analysis of *Brand, Ghosts, Rosmersholm*, and *The Master Builder*.

ARESTAD, SVERRE:

Little Eyolf and human responsibility – in *Scandinavian Studies*, xxxii, 1960.

ARESTAD, SVERRE:

When We Dead Awaken reconsidered – in *Scandinavian Studies*, xxx, 1958.

ARUP, JENS:

On *Hedda Gabler* – in *Orbis Litteranrum*, xii, 1957.

BARRANGER, M. S.:

Ibsen's Endgame: A Reconsideration of *When We Dead Awaken* – in *Modern Drama*, 17, 1974.

BARRANGER, M. S.:

Ibsen's 'Strange Story' in *The Master Builder*. A Variation in Technique – in *Modern Drama*, 15, 1972.

BENTLEY, ERIC:

Ibsen, Pro and Con – in his *In Search of Theatre* – London, 1954. Repr. in *Discussions of Henrik Ibsen*. (ed. J. W. McFarlane) Boston, 1962 – Essay on the realistic plays.

BENTLEY, ERIC:

Ibsen, Shaw, Brecht. Three Stages – in *The Rarer Action. Essays in Honour of Francis Fergusson* – (eds. A. Cheuse and R. Koffler) New Brunswick, 1970 – On *Ghosts* in particular.

BEYER, EDVARD:

When We Dead Awaken. Some notes on structure, imagery and the meaning of 'epilogue' – in *Ibsen-Årbok*, 1970/71 (*Cont. App. 2*)

BLAU, HERBERT:
Hedda Gabler, the irony of decadence – in *Educational Theatre Journal*, v, 1953.

BOLCKMANS, ALEX:
Discussion on *The Master Builder* – in *Ibsen-Årbok*, 1975/76. (*Cont. App. 3*)

BORDINAT, P.:
The dramatic function of Aunt Rina in H. Ibsen's *Hedda Gabler* – in *Studies in the Humanities*, 4.

BREITBART, SARA:
Hedda Gabler; a critical analysis – in *American Journal of Psychoanalysis*, v, 1948.

BROOKS, CLEANTH AND HEILMAN, ROBERT B.:
Rosmersholm – in their *Understanding Drama* – New York, 1945.

BROOKS, HAROLD F.:
Pygmalion and *When We Dead Awaken* – in *Notes and Queries*, 1960.

CARLSON, M.:
Patterns of Structure and Character in Ibsen's *Rosmersholm* – in *Modern Drama*, 17, 1974.

CHAMBERLAIN, JOHN S.:
Gengangere and Emigrantlitteraturen – in *Scandinavica*, 16, 1977 – Analyses the basic thematic links between *Ghosts* and Brandes' Emigrantlitteraturen.

CHAMBERLAIN, J. S.:
Tragic heroism in *Rosmersholm* – in *Modern Drama*, 17, 1974 – On the characters Rosmer and Rebecca.

CLANCY, J. H.:
Hedda Gabler; poetry in action and in object – in *Studies in Theatre and Drama*. (ed. O. G. Brockett) The Hague, 1972 – Emphasizes the non-verbal elements in the play.

CHAMBERLAIN, J. S.:
Ibsen's *Vildanden* in relation to G. Brandes' *Gustave*

Flaubert and Flaubert's *Un Coeur Simple* – in *Scandinavia*, 14, 1975.

CRAIG, GORDON:

A note on *Rosmersholm* – in *Teatro della Pergola*, Florence, Dec. 1906.

― DATALLER, ROGER:

A Doll's House – in his *Drama and Life* – London, 1938.

DAVIS, D. R.:

The death of the artist's father: Henrik Ibsen – in *The British Journal of Medical Psychology*, 46, 1973 – On *Ghosts* and *The Wild Duck*. Sees these plays in relation to the impact on the author of the death of his father in 1877.

DOWNS, BRIAN W.:

A study of Six Plays by Ibsen – Cambridge, 1950 – On *Love's Comedy*, *Brand*, *Peer Gynt*, *A Doll's House*, *The Wild Duck*, and *The Master Builder*.

DURBACH, E.:

The apotheosis of *Hedda Gabler* – in *Scandinavian Studies*, 43, 1973.

DURBACH, E.:

Sacrifice and absurdity in *The Wild Duck* – in *Mosaic*, 7, 1975.

EWBANK, INGA-STINA:

More Pregnantly than Words: some uses and Limitations of Visual Symbolism – in *Shakespeare Survey*, 24, 1971 – On I. Bergman's production of *Hedda Gabler* at the National Theatre, London.

FERGUSSON, FRANCIS:

The Idea of a Theatre – Princeton U.P. and London, 1949. Repr. in *Discussions of Henrik Ibsen*. (ed. J. W. Mc-Farlane) Boston, 1962. Also in *Ibsen. A collection of Critical Essays*. (ed. Rolf Fjelde) New Jersey, 1965 – With special reference to *Ghosts*.

FERGUSSON,FRANCIS:
The Lady from the Sea – in *Ibsen-Årbok*, 1965/66. (*Cont.*
App. 1)

FIELDS, B. S. JR.:
Ibsen's *Ghosts*: Repetitions and Repetitions – in *Papers on Language and Literature*, South Ill., 8, Supplement, Fall 1972 – On the language of *Ghosts*.

GASKELL, RONALD:
Ibsen: *Rosmersholm* – in his *Drama and Reality. The European Theatre since Ibsen* – London, 1972.

GILMAN, R.:
Henrik Ibsen: The Drawing Room and Beyond – in his *Common and Uncommon Masks. Writings on Theatre 1961–1970* – New York, 1970 – On *Rosmersholm*.

GRAIN, FRANCES:
The interpersonal psychology of some of Ibsen's later plays – in *Ibsen-Årbok*, 1974 – A Laingian analysis of the characters of the late prose plays from *The Wild Duck* to *The Master Builder*.

GRANVILLE-BARKER, HARLEY:
Ibsen and his *Rosmersholm* – in *The Use of Drama*, lectures given at Princeton University 1944. Publ. London, 1946.

GRAY, RONALD:
Ibsen; a dissenting view. A study of the last Twelve Plays – Cambridge, 1978 – Analyses the weaknesses in dramatic technique, characterization, structure and language. Contests the claim that, in the original, all Ibsen's works are forms of poetry.

GREENE, DAVID:
Reality and the heroic pattern. Last plays of Ibsen, Shakespeare, and Sophocles – Chicago, 1967.

GRUENBERG, SIDONIA M.:
The Lady from the Sea – in *Psyche*, ix, Jan. 1929.

GRUMMAN, PAUL HENRY:
Ibsen's symbolism in *The Master Builder* and *When We*

Dead Awaken – in *Nebraska University Studies*, Lincoln, x, 1910.

GUTHRIE, KARL S.:
Analysis of *The Wild Duck* – in his *Modern Tragi-comedy* – New York, 1966.

HAAKONSEN, DANIEL:
The function of sacrifice in Ibsen's realistic Plays – in *Ibsen-Årbok*, 1965/66 (*Cont. App. 1*) – Mainly on *Ghosts*.

HAAKONSEN, DANIEL:
The play-within-the-play in Ibsen's Realistic Drama – in *Ibsen-Årbok*, 1970/71 (*Cont. App. 2*)

HALLETT, C. A.:
The Wild Duck and critical cliché – in *Papers on Language and Literature*, 11 – A re-appraisal of the play, placing Gregers at the centre of tragic action and seeing Dr Relling as another 'wild duck', rather than the mouthpiece of the author.

HARDWICK, E.:
Ibsen's women – in *Seduction and Betrayal. Women and Literature* – London, 1974 – Three essays on *A Doll's House*, *Hedda Gabler* and The Rosmersholm Triangle.

HINDEN, M.:
Ibsen and Nietzsche: A Reading of *The Master Builder* – in *Modern Drama*, 15, 1972/73.

HOLTAN, ORLEY J.:
Mythic Patterns in Ibsen's Last Plays – Minneapolis, 1970 – On the plays from *The Wild Duck* to *When We Dead Awaken*.

HURT, J.:
Catiline's Dream. An Essay on Ibsen's Plays – Illinois, 1972.

JAMES, HENRY:
John Gabriel Borkman – in *Harpers Weekly*, Feb. 6, 1897. Repr. in *The Scenic Art*. (ed. Allan Wade) London, 1949.

JAMES, HENRY:
Little Eyolf – in *Harpers Weekly*, Jan. 23, 1897. Repr. in
The Scenic Art (see above).

JAMES, HENRY:
The Master Builder – in *Pall Mall Gazette*, Feb. 17, 1883.
Repr. in *The Scenic Art* (see above).

JAMES HENRY:
On the occasion of *Hedda Gabler* – in *New Review*, 1891.
Repr. in *The Scenic Art* (see above). Also repr. in *Discussions of Henrik Ibsen*. (ed. J. W. McFarlane) Boston, 1962.

JOHNSTON, BRIAN:
The Corpse and the Cargo; the Hegelian past in Ibsen's
Naturalistic Cycle – in *The Drama Review*, XIII, 1968.

JOHNSTON, BRIAN:
The Ibsen Cycle. The Design of the Plays from *Pillars of Society* to *When We Dead Awaken* – New York.

JOHNSTON, BRIAN:
The metaphoric structure of *The Wild Duck* – in *Ibsen-Årbok*, 1965/66. (*Cont. App. 1*)

KAASA, H.:
Ibsen and the Theologians – in *Scandinavian Studies*, 43,
1971 – On I's. attitude to religion and theologians, also
on the attitude of the contemporary public to his prose
plays.

KAUFMAN, M. W.:
Nietzsche, Georg Brandes and Ibsen's *The Master Builder*
– in *Comparative Drama*, 6.

KINCK, B. M.:
Laura Kieler; the model for Ibsen's Nora – in *London Mercury*, Nov. 1937 – On *A Doll's House*.

KITTANG, ATLE:
The Pretenders – Historical Vision or Psychological
Tragedy? – in *Ibsen-Årbok*, 1975/76. (*Cont. App. 3*)

KRUTCH, JOSEPH WOOD:
The Tragic Fallacy – in *Atlantic*, 142, 1928 – On *Ghosts*.

KRUUSE, J.:
The Function of Humour in the Later Plays of Ibsen – in
Ibsen-Årbok, 1970/71. (*Cont. App. 2*)

LEE, JEANETTE:
The Ibsen Secret; A key to the prose dramas of Henrik Ibsen –
London, 1907.

LELAND, C. W.:
Ghosts seen from an existential aspect – in *Ibsen-Årbok*,
1974.

LOGEMANN, H.:
A Commentary on Henrik Ibsen's Peer Gynt – *its language,
literary associations and folklore* – Haag, 1917.

LOWENTHAL, LEO:
Motifs in the Realistic Plays – in his *Literature and the
Image of Man* – Boston, 1957. Repr. in *Ibsen. A Collection of
Critical Essays*. (ed. R. Fjelde) New Jersey, 1965.

LYONS, CHARLES R.:
The Function of Dream and Reality in *John Gabriel
Borkman* – in *Scandinavian Studies*, 45, 1973.

LYONS, CHARLES R.:
The Master Builder as Drama of the Self – in *Scandinavian
Studies*, 39, 1967.

LYONS, CHARLES R.:
Henrik Ibsen. The Divided Consciousness – Southern Illinois,
1972.

McCARTHY, MARY:
The Will and Testament of Ibsen – in her *Sight and
Spectacles* – London, 1958 – On *The Wild Duck*.

McFARLANE, JAMES W.:
Hauptmann, Ibsen and the Concept of Naturalism – in
Hauptmann Centenary Lecture, publ. by Inst. Germanic
Studies, London, 1964.

McFARLANE, JAMES W.:
Meaning and Evidence in Ibsen's Drama – in *Ibsen-Årbok*,

1965/66. (*Cont. App. 1*) – On *The Pillars of Society* and *Rosmersholm*.

MAILLY, WILLIAM:
Henrik Ibsen's *The Master Builder* – in *Arena*, Boston, xxxix, 1908.

MARKER, LISE LONE AND MARKER, F. J.:
William Bloch and Naturalism in the Scandinavian Theatre – in *Theatre Survey*, 15 – On *An Enemy of the People*, the production at the Royal Danish Theatre in Copenhagen 1883.

MAYERSON, CAROLINE W.:
Thematic symbols in *Hedda Gabler* – in *Scandinavian Studies and Notes*, xxii, 1950. Repr. in *Ibsen. A collection of Critical Essays*. (ed. R. Fjelde) New Jersey, 1965.

MENCKEN, H. L.:
History of *A Doll's House* – in *Theatre*, New York, xii, 1910.

MORI, MITSUYA:
Ibsen's Dramatic Irony – in *Ibsen-Årbok*, 1970/71. (*Cont. App. 2*) – On the dramatic irony in *Ghosts* and *The Wild Duck*.

MUIR, KENNETH:
Last periods of Shakespeare, Racine, Ibsen – Liverpool, 1961.

NORTHAM, JOHN:
Dividing Worlds – Oslo/New York, 1965 – On *Rosmersholm* and *The Tempest*.

NORTHAM, JOHN:
Ibsen. A Critical Study – Cambridge, 1973 – On the heroic in *The Comedy of Love, Brand, Ghosts, The Wild Duck, Hedda Gabler*, and *Little Eyolf*.

NORTHAM, JOHN:
Ibsen's Dramatic Method: A study of the prose dramas – London, 1953.

NORTHAM, JOHN:
Ibsen's search for the hero – in *Edda*, LX, 1960. Repr. in

Ibsen. A collection of Critical Essays. (ed. R. Fjelde) New Jersey, 1965 – Mainly on the prose plays, particularly *A Doll's House*, in which Nora is seen as 'a modern individual and a heroine'.

NORTHAM, JOHN:
Some Uses of Rhetoric in *Ghosts* – in *Ibsen-Årbok*, 1971/72.

NORTHAM, JOHN:
The Substance of Ibsen's Idealism – in *Ibsen-Årbok* 1965/66. (*Cont. App. 1*) – On the idealism and heroism of the basically non-heroic characters in Ibsen's prose plays.

OSTER, ROSE-MARIE G.:
Do We Dead Awaken? Ibsen as Social Psychologist – in *Educational Theatre Journal*, 22, 1970 – Underlines the mental evasiveness and unconscious life of Ibsen's protagonists.

PEARCE, JOHN CALVIN:
Hegelian ideas in three tragedies by Ibsen – in *Scandinavian Studies*, XXXIV, 1962 – On the Hegelian ideas in *Catiline, The Pretenders*, and *Emperor and Galilean*.

RAPHAEL, ROBERT:
From *Hedda Gabler* to *When We Dead Awaken*; the quest for self-realisation – in *Scandinavian Studies*, xxxvi, 1964.

REED, ROBERT R.:
Rebecca of Manningtree and Ibsen's Rebecca West – in *Notes and Queries*, Nov., 1957 – On *Rosmersholm*.

REICHARDT, KONSTANTIN:
Tragedy of Idealism – in *Tragic Themes in Western Literature*. (ed. C. Brooks) New Haven, 1955, new ed. 1964 – On *Rosmersholm*.

REINERT, OTTO:
Sight Imagery in *The Wild Duck* – in *Journal of English and Germanic Phil.*, iv, 1956.

RICHARDSON, J.:
Ibsen's Nora and Ours – in *Commentary*, July, 1971.

RIVICER, JOAN:
The inner world of Ibsen's *The Master Builder* – in *International Journal of Psycho-analysis*, xxxii, 1952.

ROBERTS, MARK:
Harps in the Air; the Sublime Discontent of Bygmester Solness – in his *The Tradition of Romantic Morality* – London, 1971 – On *The Master Builder*.

ROGERS, K. M.:
— A woman appreciates Ibsen – in *The Centennial Review*, 18 – Surveys the feminism introduced into the later plays and developed fully in *A Doll's House* and *Ghosts*.

RORRISON, H.:
Berlin democratic theatre and its *Peer Gynt* – in *Theatre Quarterly*, 4, no. 1.

RØED, ARNE:
The crutch is floating – in *Ibsen-Årbok*, 1974 – A psychological analysis of the characters in *Little Eyolf*.

RØNNING, HELGE:
Individualism and the Liberal Dilemma. Notes towards a Sociological Interpretation of *An Enemy of the People* by Henrik Ibsen – in *Ibsen-Årbok*, 1975/76. (*Cont. App. 3*)

RUUD, M. B.:
Ibsen's Kjæmpehøien – in *Scandinavian Studies and Notes*, VI, 1918/19 – On *The Burial Mound*.

SCHATIA, VIVA:
Hedda Gabler's *A Doll's House* – in *Psychoanalytical Review*, xxvi, 1938.

SCHATIA, VIVA:
The Master Builder, a case of involutal psychosis – in *Psychoanalytical Review*, xxvii, 1940.

SHATZY, J.:
Heredity as a metaphor in Ibsen's plays – in *Edda*, 74, 1974 – On *A Doll's House* and *Ghosts*.

SHIPLEY, JOSEPH T.:
Five Major Plays – in *Analytical Notes and Review*, New York, 1965.

SPRINCHORN, E.:
   Ibsen and the Immoralists – in *Comparative Literature Studies*.
   9, 1972 – On *Hedda Gabler*. Sees Løvborg as created in
   the double image of Georg Brandes and Friedrich
   Nietzsche, and Hedda as a projection of Henrik Ibsen
   himself.
STEENE, BIRGITTA:
   Macbeth and *Rosmersholm*: a comparison – in *Proceedings
   of the Fifth International Study Conference on Scand. Lit.*,
   London, 1964.
STENBERG, T. T.:
   Ibsen's *Catilina* and Goethe's *Iphigenie auf Tauris* – in
   Modern Language Notes, xxxix, 1924.
STØVERUD, TORBJØRM:
   The Wild Duck – A Study in Ambiguity – in his *Mile-
   stones of Norwegian Literature*, Oslo, 1967.
TENNANT, P. D. F.:
   A Critical Study of the Composition of Ibsen's *Vildanden*
   – in *Edda*, xxxiv, 1934 – On *The Wild Duck*.
THOMAS, DAVID:
   Patterns of interactions in Ibsen's *Ghosts* – in *Ibsen-
   Årbok*, 1974.
THUNE, E.:
   The paradox of the Boyg: a study of Peer Gynt's human-
   ization – in *Modern Drama*, 19, 1975 – Attempts to throw
   light on the Boyg–Peer relationship by pointing to parallel
   situations in Shakespeare's plays.
TÖRNQUIST, E.:
   The Illness Pattern in *The Master Builder* – in *Scandinavica*,
   11, 1972.
TÖRNQUIST, E.:
   Individualism in *The Master Builder* – in *Ibsen-Årbok*,
   1975/76. (*Cont. App. 3*)
VAN LAAN, THOMAS:
   Language in *Vildanden* – in *Ibsen-Årbok*, 1974.

VAN LAAN, THOMAS:
The Idiom of Drama – London, 1970 – On *Rosmersholm*.

WATTS, C. T.:
The Unseen Catastrophe in Ibsen's *Vildanden* – in *Scandinavica*, 12, 1973 – On *The Wild Duck*.

WEBB, E.:
The ambiguities of secularization: modern transformations of the kingdom in Nietzsche, Ibsen, Beckett, and Stevens – in his *The Dark Dove: The Sacred and Secular in Modern Literature* – Seattle/Washington U.P., 1975 – On *Hedda Gabler*.

WEBB, E.:
The Radical Irony of *Hedda Gabler* – in *Modern Lang. Quarterly*, 31, 1970.

WEIGAND, HERMANN:
The Modern Ibsen – a Reconsideration – New York, 1925, new ed. 1960 – On the prose plays.

WICKSTED, PHILIP H.:
Four lectures on Henrik Ibsen dealing chiefly with his metrical works – London, 1892.

WILSON, EDMUND:
Ghosts – in *Literary Review*, iv, 1924.

WISDOM, JO:
The lust for power in *Hedda Gabler* – in *Psychoanalytical Review*, xxxi, 4, Oct., 1944.

ZENTNER, JULES:
Figures of estrangement – Peer Gynt's other selves – in *Edda*, 73, 1971.

ZENTNER, JULES:
Ibsen's protagonists – Their personal and social responsibilities – in *Ibsen-Årbok*, 1965/66. (*Cont. App. 1*) – Analyses I.'s Protagonists in his last twelve plays, their striving for self-realization, tragedy and death.

ZUCKER, A. E.:
Ibsen: The Master Builder – London, 1930.